In THE STEPS *of* · THOMAS HARDY

ANNE-MARIE EDWARDS

Photographs by Mike Edwards

COUNTRYSIDE BOOKS
Newbury, Berkshire

Also in this series:
In the Steps of Jane Austen
In the Steps of the Brontës

First published under the title
Discovering Hardy's Wessex 1978
This revised and expanded edition published 1995
Revised and reprinted 2000
© Anne-Marie Edwards 1989

COUNTRYSIDE BOOKS
3 CATHERINE ROAD
NEWBURY, BERKSHIRE

To view our complete range of books,
please visit us at
www.countrysidebooks.co.uk

ISBN 1 85306 047 X

Maps drawn by Julie Edwards, based on Ordnance Survey Maps
with the permission of the Controller of Her Majesty's Stationery Office.
Crown Copyright reserved.

Portrait of Thomas Hardy on the front cover and photographs on pages 15, 16,
38, 186, are reproduced by kind permission of the Dorset Natural History and
Archaeological Society, Dorset County Museum.

Line drawings are engravings by Thomas Bewick
Cover illustration of the White Horse by Harry Ashley

Produced through MRM Associates Ltd., Reading
Printed in England

Contents

The statue of Thomas Hardy at Top o'Town, Dorchester. The wild plants around his feet represent the Dorset heathlands which he immortalised as 'Egdon'.

Acknowledgements

It is a pleasure to thank all the people who have helped me – especially the staff of Southampton, Hythe and Totton public libraries, Mr R. N. R. Peers, the Curator of Dorset County Museum, and Mrs Ruth Wood who gave me valuable information about Dorchester's Mill Street Housing Society. For help with checking the routes I am grateful to the Ramblers' Association, particularly Bill Myers, Anthony Hawkey, Alfred Palmer and Alan Mattingly, and to the Backpackers Club for their interest and support. I received assistance also from the County Surveyor for Cornwall and the County Surveyor for Dorset, and the Principal of the Dorset College of Agriculture at Kingston Maurward. I thank the Thomas Hardy Society for their help. The Society publishes Tour guides to the novels. Membership of the Society is open to all and details may be obtained from the Hon. Secretary: Mrs K. Fowler, Park Farm, Tolpuddle, Dorchester, Dorset DT2 7HG.

I would like to thank all my good friends at Radio Solent and BBC Publications for their help and encouragement in compiling the first edition. For help with the research needed for this third edition I am delighted to be able to thank Mr Robert Dorey of Kingston, near Corfe. I am grateful also for the detailed advance information on new road networks very kindly supplied to me by Mr Hutchinson, County Surveyor, Dorset County Council and Mr Luxmoore. It is a pleasure also to thank Nicholas and Suzanne Battle of Countryside Books for their interest and enthusiastic support.

My thanks to good friends who have patiently walked with me especially Mary, whose cheerfulness smooths away all difficulties. Finally I thank my splendid family: Julie who drew the maps, Chris and Joanne, and my husband Mike who took the photographs.

Ashurst, 1995

Preface
by
Trevor Johnson

writer and lecturer on Thomas Hardy

It is a pleasure to welcome this revised and enlarged edition of Anne Marie Edwards' book. My wife and I have made good use of its predecessors; indeed the original paper-back has now retired hurt. There are some 'superior persons' who profess themselves immune to the charm of such books as this: they don't want to trace William and Dorothy Wordsworth 'home at Grasmere', or follow Sir Walter Scott's footsteps through the Eildon Hills. No guide books, they would say, are needed for the country of the mind. Hardy certainly did not share this puritanical persuasion: he felt that there was what he once termed a 'memorial presence' in places like Keats's house in Hampstead, asking the poet's shade,

> Will you wake wind-wafts on the stairs?
> Swing the doors open noisily?
> Stand as an umbraged ghost beside
>   Your ancient tree?

Certainly we shall still find many traces of Hardy's spirit in the land that made him, that he loved and walked or cycled over until well into his seventies; the raw material of the fictive realm he re-christened Wessex. And, as Belloc said,

> He does not die that can bequeath
> Some influence to the land he loves,

But what of his imagined country and its people? Well, to begin with, much of it isn't imaginary at all in the same way as Tolkien's *Middle Earth*. Nearly all his natural features keep their original designations and, however redolent of

Hardy they may now seem, *Crimmercrock Lane* and *Dogbury Gate* are ancient names, not of his coinage. Indeed, he said that his 'landscape, prehistoric antiquities . . . and old English architecture' were all 'done from the real', while, where towns and villages are concerned, though 'no detail is guaranteed', most were 'suggested by certain real places'. He even helped Hermann Lea to identify a good few of them. So, if with Anne-Marie's help we set out to find them, we can be confident of the goodwill of his shade. Where his people are concerned perhaps all we can hope for is to meet their lineal descendants; Jan Coggan can still be encountered in Dorset pubs. But for their 'close inter-social relations and eccentric individuals' the essential conditions are attachment to the soil of one particular spot by generation after generation, and that had already ended in Hardy's own day.

There are several guides to Hardy's topography; indeed the first appeared nearly ninety years ago. But this one has the salient advantage over all the others that it is meant to go into an anorak pocket, not lie on a coffee-table. The walker who uses it can tramp over the same 'drongs' as Hardy daily trudged from Bockhampton to Dorchester, even – in season – getting his boots similarly 'mire-bestarred'. And, as he does so, over and above the Hardy connection, he will travel over landscapes which, Hardy maintained, 'cannot be regarded as inferior to any inland scenery in the West of England, or perhaps anywhere.' More than one might hope, that is still true today.

Lastly, a word from the viewpoint of the reader. This book, for anyone familiar with Hardy's writings, can perform two further valuable functions. In enabling us to compare the words on his page with *The Place on the Map* (a characteristic poem-title) it allows us to see how 'Long looking, long loving, long desiring: these win at length to the inmost heart of a thing', as Walter de la Mare, a great admirer of Hardy, said of Edward Thomas, another.

But even more importantly, it may help to add a dimension to our own feeling for place. Suppose we use it to follow the lovely and (thanks to the National Trust) unspoiled Valency Valley from St. Juliot to Boscastle (Hardy's *Castle Boterel*). We shall tread the same path as Hardy and Emma Gifford on that day in 1870 when they

> Walked under a sky
> Of blue with a leaf-wove awning of green
> In the burn of August to paint the scene,

to reach the point where by 'the purl of a little valley fall' they stopped to picnic and, washing up their shared wine-glass in the cascade, 'It slipped and sank, and was past recall.' Now, to anyone who has read the marvellous poem *Under the Waterfall* from which these extracts come, and consequently is aware that – 'Though where precisely none ever has known' – 'There the glass still is jammed darkly, nothing to show how prized,' and also that, as the poem ends

> No lip has touched it since his and mine
> In turns therefrom sipped lovers' wine.

then to stand and look at the 'runlet that never ceases,' and listen as

> With a hollow boiling voice it speaks
> And has spoken since hills were turfless peaks.

is to have an experience almost luminous in its intensity. Of course, I cannot guarantee such 'moments of vision' as Hardy called them. But even one will more than repay you the cost of this book, whose author, though no one could miss her enthusiasm, never gets between the reader and the Hardy scene, and whose husband's photographs are an additional delight.

Trevor Johnson
Dunscar, Lancs.
May 1989

Introduction

Thomas Hardy is recognised throughout the world as one of England's greatest writers, timeless and universal in his appeal. Like many writers he can enthral and delight us but his work has a special quality: a mark of genius. He has the power to win our hearts. What is the secret of this quiet countryman who wished to be remembered as a man who noticed little things? He writes with love and concern about what he knows. So keen is his observation and so vivid his description of the southern countryside and its people during the early years of Queen Victoria's reign that we are drawn into the world he creates; we care about his characters.

At first glance Hardy may appear to have set his novels in a bewilderingly large area and the fact that he gives his own names to many places may add to our possible confusion. But viewed in the perspective of Hardy's life, his Wessex – his literary world, always drawn, as he said, 'from the real' – assumes its own shape and meaning. That is the aim of this book. I have set out to walk in Hardy's own footsteps and those of his characters following the ancient ways they followed in the course of their everyday lives: to work, to church, to the nearest pub, and between neighbouring villages. These routes, preserved by use, are now our rights of way. With Hardy as my guide I have found to my delight that his beautiful Wessex still exists. We can still walk in his world today.

Anne-Marie Edwards

Trevor Johnson, inv. & scrips.

S. Wales

Thoma[s]
WE[SSEX]
a new map [of]
novels & po[ems]

R. SEVERN

Badminton

Bristol

Bath

The Bristol Channel

OUTER WESSEX

Priddy

the Mendips

Dunkery Tor

Markton

Stancy Castle

Wylls Neck

Gurney Slade

Fountall

Vobster

Falls

QUEEN'S SEDGE MOOR

Glaston

Marshall's Elm

R. PARRET

Keinton Mandeville

Part of Lyonesse, N. Cornwall.

TONEBOROUGH
DEANE

The Atlantic
OCEAN
Stratleigh

Part of
Lower
WESSEX
Stretton

Part
of
Exon
Moor

High Cliff
Beeny Cliff
Targan Bay
Castle Boterel
Bossiny
Dun-
nagel

Barret Down

Toneborough

Ivelchester

Camelot

Cortch Hill

Tintinhull

Narrobourne

Ivell

Sherton Abbas

The Hintocks

S. WESSEX

Bullbarrow

N. & E. Endelstow

Otterham

Penpethy
Camelton
Boutor

St. Cleather
St. Launce's

Chard

Crewkerne

Eversheaḍ

Dilsdon Den

Emmin-
ster

Abbots
Cernel

Exonbury

R. ?

Axmouth

R. FROOM

Weatherbury

Casterbridge

Mellst[ock]

Topsham

R. EX ?

R. ? CHARD ?

Port Bredy

Blackon

Overcom[be]

LOWER
WESSEX

CHESIL BANK

Dead Man's Bay

Budmouth

The English
Channel

The Isl[e]
Sylva[?]

The Beal

The [?]

Hardy's [WESS]EX

...realm of his...
MLXXXII.

N

W — E

S

1515 · Christminster
Lumsdon · · Osney
· Cowley

R. THAMES

N. WESSEX

ICKNIELD WAY .... · Alfredston

Marlbury Downs
Cresscombe · · Fenworth
·le Combe · · The Brown House
· Chippenham · Chaddleworth · Marygreen
vick Ho. · Clatford Ho. · Marlbury
s-WESSEX · · R. KENNET · Sulhampstead Abbots · Theale · Aldbrickham
· Kennetbridge · · Shinfield
Tottenham Ho. · Angpen Beacon
· Burbidge
THE GREAT PLAIN
R. AVON
Stoke Barehills · Old Basing Ho.
· Quartershot
Jarminster · Weydon Priors · Herriard · Herriard Ho.
Stonehenge
· Amesbury
ton ·
UPPER WESSEX
R. TEST
· Wintoncester
fonthill Abbey · Wilton Ho. · Melchester · West Hill
The Manor Court · Woodyates · Fernel Hall · Romsey · Marwell Old Hall
Arrowthorne Lodge · Deansleigh Park
Chaseborough · Fordingbridge · Southampton
Trantridge
· Bramsbury Court
THE GREAT FOREST
Portsmouth
s Co't Rookington House
Warborne · Solentsea
· Havenpool · Ryde
· Sandbourne
The Island

DLE
elbridge
Corvesgate
d
ngers
tle
es
Knollsea
Durlston Head
St. Aldhelm's Head

SUSSEX

Calendar

1805 Nelson's victory over the French and Spanish fleets at Trafalgar ended the threat of a landing by the French at Weymouth. (Hardy set *The Trumpet Major* against this background.) – **1810** Macadam began the construction of good roads – **1815** Napoleon finally defeated at Waterloo. (Hardy visited veterans of the battle and gathered material for *The Dynasts*). Corn Law passed by Parliament prohibiting the importation of foreign corn until British corn reached 80s a quarter. (This act influenced the economic background of *The Mayor of Casterbridge*.) A long period of acute distress and unrest followed. – **1825** Opening of Stockton-Darlington railway, the first passenger line. (As railways developed rapidly greater mobility became possible for all classes in society creating problems which Hardy depicts in his novels.) – **1830** Agricultural labourers' riots in the south – **1832** First Parliamentary Reform Act – **1834** The Tolpuddle martyrs. Six Dorset men were transported for trying to form a union – **1837** Accession of Queen Victoria – Charles Dickens: *Pickwick Papers* and *Oliver Twist* – **1840** Harrison Ainsworth: *The Tower of London*. (Hardy enjoyed his romances.) – **1846** Repeal of the Corn laws – **1848** John Stuart Mill: *Political Economy* – **1850** Invention of steam threshing machine (Hardy shows the impact of machines on workers unaccustomed to them in *Tess of the d'Urbervilles*.) – **1857** Herbert Spencer (philosopher and social scientist): *Essays* – **1858** Royal Opera House, London, opened at Covent Garden – **1859** Charles Darwin: *The Origin of Species*. Made an enormous impact on modern thought. – **1860** Wilkie Collins: *Woman in White*. (Hardy was advised to write in a similar style. The result was *Desperate Remedies*.) – **1866** Algernon Charles Swinburne: *Poems and Ballads*. (Hardy identified with him in rebelling against class distinctions.) – **1870** Outbreak of Franco-Prussian war – **1871** Trade Union Act: Unions given full legal recognition – **1873** Agricultural and industrial depression – **1875** Disraeli's social reforms – **1878** Red Flag Act: mechanical road vehicles not to exceed 4mph and to be preceded by man with a red flag – **1884** Third Reform Act gave agricultural labourers the right to vote – **1885** The Rover Co. marketed Lawson's bicycle chain-driven to back wheel. (Hardy and Emma were keen cyclists, exploring the countryside around Dorchester.) – **1901** Accession of Edward VII – **1903** Women's Union formed to demand votes for women. First flight by Orville and Wilbur Wright. Henry Ford founded his motor company. – **1910** Accession of George V – **1913** D. H. Lawrence: *Sons and Lovers*. (He owed a debt to Hardy for extending the confines of the novel.) **1914–18** World War 1. – **1922** T. S. Eliot: *The Waste Land* – **1927** Virginia Woolf: *To the Light-house*. (A novel in which a character's thoughts rather than his actions are emphasised. Hardy was moving towards this in *The Well-Beloved*.)

1840	Thomas Hardy was born the son of a master mason, in a cottage at Higher Bockhampton, a small village about three miles east of Dorchester. The cottage faced the pastoral valley of the Frome which features so often in his work. Directly behind the cottage rose a large expanse of wild and open heathland which he immortalised as 'Egdon Heath'. From his bedroom window he could see the memorial to Admiral Hardy, captain of HMS *Victory*, on Black Down. Hardy's lifelong interest in the Napoleonic wars was also fostered by his paternal grandmother's recollections and his discovery of a periodical *A History of the Wars*. His father shared with his son a love of music, particularly old ballads, and his mother, Jemima, encouraged him to read and study, especially the classics.
1848	Hardy attended the village school in Lower Bockhampton which had been established by the local lady of the manor, Julia Augusta Martin of Kingston Maurward. She took a special interest in him.
1849–1856	Jemima, hearing that the headmaster of a school in Dorchester was an excellent Classics teacher, transferred him there from the village school. Hardy learned Latin, played the fiddle at weddings and dances and shyly admired the pretty girls, especially Louisa Harding whom he never forgot although his only words to her were 'Good Evening'.
1856–1861	After leaving school, Hardy was articled to John Hicks, a Dorchester architect and church restorer. He continued his study of the Latin classics in the early morning and began to study Greek. He witnessed the public execution of a woman on the roof of Dorchester gaol – a scene which stayed with him for the rest of his life and contributed to the final scene of *Tess of the d'Urbervilles*. He began writing verse and was much influenced by modern thinking which threatened many accepted religious beliefs.
1862–1867	Hardy moved to London to work for the architect Arthur Blomfield. He danced, enjoyed music, studied the old masters in the National Gallery and read widely, both poetry and politics. But he disliked London society with its rigid class system and, worn down, he returned home.
1867–1870	Hicks re-employed Hardy to work on church restoration. He completed his first novel *The Poor Man and the Lady*. (Since destroyed but containing passages sharply critical of London society.) He began writing *Desperate Remedies*, a thriller with a complicated plot. In March 1870 Hardy was sent by Crickmay, Hicks' successor, to St Juliot in Cornwall to draw up plans for the restoration of the church. Here he met Emma Lavinia Gifford. They fell almost immediately in love.
1871	*Desperate Remedies* was published and met with a mixed reception. Always senstive to criticism, Hardy was so upset

by one review that he said 'he wished he were dead.' He turned to characters and themes that were familiar to him and wrote *Under the Greenwood Tree*. With Emma's encouragement later in the year he began *A Pair of Blue Eyes*.

1872 *Under the Greenwood Tree* was published and well received. He continued writing *A Pair of Blue Eyes* and agreed to its serialization in *Tinsley's Magazine*.

1873–1874 Leslie Stephen invited Hardy to write a serial for his prestigious *Cornhill* magazine. *Far from the Madding Crowd* was a success and in September 1874 Hardy and Emma were married in London. Leslie Stephen asked Hardy for another novel and he began *The Hand of Ethelberta*.

1875–1878 *The Hand of Ethelberta* was serialized in *Cornhill* and proved disappointing. In 1876 the Hardys moved to Riverside Villa in Sturminster Newton where they were very happy. Hardy wrote several poems about Sturminster and, recalling the heath at Bockhampton, *The Return of the Native*. He began more extensive study of the Napoleonic wars.

1878–1881 In March the Hardys moved back to London. Hardy continued his researches in the British Museum for *The Trumpet Major* set in 1804–5. The novel was serialised in 1880. Hardy was now becoming well known. He fell very seriously ill after beginning his next novel *A Laodicean* and was forced to dictate the story to Emma from his sickbed.

1881–1882 Hardy recovered and in May 1881 they moved to Wimborne Minster. He began *Two on a Tower* which appeared in the *Atlantic Monthly* from May to December 1882.

1883 Emma and Hardy moved to a house in the centre of Dorchester.

1884–1887 Dorchester inspired its own novel set in the years before the repeal of the Corn Laws. Hardy wrote *The Mayor of Casterbridge* 'off and on' as he said, finishing the story in April 1885. It was serialized during the early part of 1886 on both sides of the Atlantic, in *The Graphic* and *Harper's Weekly*. In June 1885 Hardy and Emma moved into a home of their own at last, Max Gate, close to Dorchester. He began *The Woodlanders* in 1886 and finished the story in February 1887. The novel appeared in *Macmillan's Magazine*, and in *Harper's Bazaar* in America.

1888–1891 During this time Hardy wrote many short stories. After much adaptation to suit accepted Victorian ideas of morality he finished his next novel *Tess of the d'Urbervilles* by the end of 1890 to be published in *The Graphic* and *Harper's Bazaar* from July to December 1891. *Tess*, though liked by many, created a storm of protest and criticism which affected Hardy deeply.

1892–1896 Perhaps as an interlude between two great novels Hardy wrote *The Well-Beloved*, which was serialized in *The Illustrated London News* and *Harper's Bazaar*. His marrige was becoming increasingly unhappy. Emma objected to his ideas in his next novel *Jude the Obscure*. The story was published in *Harper's New Monthly Magazine* from December 1894 to November 1895. So bitter was the criticism that Hardy resolved to give up novel writing and return to writing poetry. He had always considered his verse 'the better part of me'.

1897–1898	Hardy wrote and revised poems for his first collection, *Wessex Poems*.
1902	His interest in the Napoleonic wars reached fruition as he began a great epic poem *The Dynasts*.
1910	The Order of Merit was conferred upon Hardy.
1912	Early in the year Hardy made his final revision of the Wessex novels. In November Emma died suddenly.
1913	Overcome with grief and remorse after the discovery of her *Recollections* recalling their courtship days, Hardy revisited St Juliot and placed a memorial tablet to her in the church. He wrote some of his finest love poetry in her memory.
1914	In February he married Florence Dugdale. At the outbreak of war he joined a group of prominent writers to support the Allied Cause.
1914–1928	Hardy published several collections of verse. He prefaced *Late Lyrics and Earlier* with a statement of his views and a strong denial of the charge that he was a pessimist. At the close of 1927 his strength was failing. On 10 January 1928 he died. His ashes were placed in Westminster Abbey and his heart buried in Emma's grave in Stinsford churchyard.

One of Hubert Herkumer's illustrations for Tess of the d'Urbervilles.

The frontispiece from the Chatto & Windus edition of Under the
Greenwood Tree *1878. The little scenes round the edges show the
church quire, Fancy at the organ. Dick and Fancy in their wagon,
carol singers and Dick & Fancy's wedding.*

1

Hardy's birthplace and 'Under the Greenwood Tree'

Walk distance: 5 miles

Perhaps more than any other writer, Hardy knew, understood and was faithful to his own countryside, particularly Dorset where he was born and lived most of his life. Dorset's windswept uplands and quiet villages tucked away beneath the downs have changed remarkably little since Hardy was born at Higher Bockhampton, near Dorchester in 1840. We can walk in Hardy's countryside today and see it much as he saw it. From the hillsides the terraces of Celtic villages still look down on square towers surrounded by clusters of thatched roofs as smoothly curved as the downs themselves. In market places we find the scalloped steps of Saxon crosses where folk still meet to buy and sell, gather the news and discuss local affairs. Mills, malthouses, smithies and bakeries stand as reminders of the days when each village was a self-sufficient community and the people, as Hardy paints them, as individual as their occupations. He pictures for us the life of these remote valleys before the impact of the railways, industrial machinery and modern thinking had greatly changed centuries-old customs, skills and beliefs. Walking in Dorset today, in the footsteps of Hardy, time, in his phrase, seems to 'close up like a fan' – past and present are one. The village musicians who in most churches once formed their quire of violins, serpents, oboes and clarinets may, as Hardy regretted, no longer be heard, but the bell ringers, still under the care of 'the steeple keeper' flourish in even the smallest community.

I would like to take you with me to the heart of Hardy's Wessex, the lonely spot 'between a heath and a wood' where he was born. Today, the cottage is still a quiet and remote place. It stands at the end of a narrow lane in Higher Bockhampton, a small village about three miles east of Dorchester. Approaching via the A35, turn right following the sign for Higher Bockhampton. After about half a mile a sign indicates Hardy's birth-place down a lane on the left. Go down the lane and turn right for the car park, a short distance further at the foot of Thorncombe Wood. This lovely wood which Hardy knew well is now a nature reserve. The walk, about five miles all the way round, begins and ends here. From the car park follow the sign for Hardy's cottage, uphill through tall oaks, beeches and sweet chestnuts. This is the countryside of one of Hardy's earliest novels, *Under the Greenwood Tree*. Hardy sets this delightful story, full of humour and lively characters directly around his home, in Higher and Lower Bockhampton and nearby Stinsford, which he calls 'Mellstock'. His people follow his own walks, around the two hamlets, along the Frome valley to church, and to Dorchester across the flat water meadows by way of Grey's bridge. And the most important characters in the story, the Dewy family, live in Hardy's house itself, only slightly veiled in early editions of the novel.

The path bears left through magnificent beeches. In his first poem, written when he was sixteen, Hardy describes his home:

> 'High beeches bending, hang a veil of boughs,
> And sweep against the roof ...'

Today, these beeches still shade the grey wall of his house which you glimpse through their branches on your left. Walk round the side of the cottage into the lane. To the right is a gate leading onto the heath which Hardy was to immortalise as 'Egdon'. The memorial to Hardy close by was placed there by some of his American admirers. Turn left down the lane

Hardy's birthplace, at Higher Bockhampton. In Under the Greenwood Tree *he describes it as 'a long low cottage with a hipped roof of thatch . . .' and rents it temporarily to the Dewy family.*

for a few yards to a wicket gate opening into the garden of the cottage. This is how Hardy describes his home – for the purposes of the story temporarily rented by the Dewy family – in *Under the Greenwood Tree*. 'It was a long low cottage with a hipped roof of thatch, having dormer windows breaking up into the eaves, a chimney standing in the middle of the ridge and another at each end.' Today, honeysuckle clambers up the walls as it did when Hardy was a boy and apple trees are still scattered in the small orchard beside the garden. The shrubs are allowed to straggle a little among colourful masses of cottage-garden flowers – marigolds, pansies, day lilies and phlox. The cottage, its homely cob walls faced with brick and rendered with cement, was built in 1800 by Thomas Hardy's great grandfather for his son, also Thomas, who was a master mason.

Inside, the cottage has changed little. From *Under the Greenwood Tree* the small room on the right 'of a character between pantry and cellar' retaining its deep bread oven, is easily identified. On the left, the stone-flagged room with its low beam bisecting the ceiling from which the mistletoe hung dangerously close to the heads of the dancers below is just as described when it served as a meeting place for the Mellstock quire and the setting for the Dewys' Christmas party. The great inglenook fireplace where the young Hardy sat enthralled listening to the country tales of his grandmother dominates the room. In the novel, Mrs. Dewy is concerned about the hams and sides of bacon which, as in all country households, are hanging in its spacious depths to smoke. Would the cheerfully blazing Christmas fire broil them?

Upstairs, in the small bedroom he shared with his brother Henry, Hardy wrote *Under the Greenwood Tree*. He liked to sit in the deep window seat with its view over the garden looking towards the monument to Admiral Hardy on Black Down. Hardy was interested in him both as a remote ancestor and for the part he played in the battle of Trafalgar as captain of Nelson's flagship *Victory*. He introduces Captain Hardy into his historical novel *The Trumpet Major*.

Just as the setting of *Under the Greenwood Tree* is drawn from life so are its characters and theme. Hardy wrote, 'I find it a great advantage to be actually among the people described at the time of describing them' and although the events in the story take place during his childhood days, it all rings wonderfully true.

The story is concerned mainly with the effect upon the local church musicians who formed the quire, of the new parson's decision to phase them out and install a fashionable organ. Here Hardy was again on home ground – his grandfather, father and uncle had been the mainstay of their local church quire at Stinsford. Although the quire was dissolved when Hardy was a child he, of course, heard many tales of their various activities and treasured their hand-made music books (which can be seen in Dorchester museum). One of the duties of the quire was to play and sing carols at Christmas and the novel describes how they met beforehand at the Dewys' house. It was a merry gathering. Meetings 'necessitated suppers and suppers demanded plenty of liquor'.

The carol singers went on to Stinsford church. We shall follow in their footsteps, taking the route which was Hardy's own way to church and to school in Dorchester. Leave the cottage by the wicket gate and turn left down the lane. Few of the old houses which formed what Hardy termed 'veteran's valley' remain. Pass the turning to the car park and walk up to a minor road straight ahead. This is Cuckoo Lane, once embowered with trees and famous for its cuckoos. Turn left along Cuckoo Lane for a few yards, until you see a farm track leading right with a bridleway sign for Stinsford. This track – known as 'the drong' in Hardy's time – is our way. Turn right and walk down the track. Directly ahead is Admiral Hardy's monument on the horizon. When the track bears right, keep straight on through a gate into a field. Cross the field, keeping the hedge (which later becomes a fence) close on your right. All around you is the curving and dipping Dorset countryside, the quiet fields and copses that Hardy knew.

From the next gate the right-of-way leads ahead over the middle of the field to the hedge on the other side. (If there is a crop you may prefer to walk round the edge of the field.) Follow the path downhill to meet a cart track. Turn left along this track which leads you through a gate to a minor road which skirts Kingston Maurward Park. Cross the road following the sign for Kingston Maurward and Lower Bockhampton. Go through the gate directly ahead to follow a tempting path over the parkland with a hedge at first on the right. This is a beautiful walk across lush meadows shaded by enormous chestnut trees. We first walked this way on a golden late August afternoon, so still that we could hear the buzzing of countless insects among the purple thistle heads and the soft brushing of their wings in the dry grass.

Soon the great house, Kingston Maurward Manor, appears clearly a little to the right. It is a solid-looking, clean-cut elegant mansion. Here lived Julia Augusta Martin who founded the village school and took a motherly interest in Hardy as a child. He never forgot her and she is probably the prototype of the many firm-willed rich ladies who figure in his stories. The manor is the 'Knapwater House' of his first published novel *Desperate Remedies* where lived the imperious Miss Aldclyffe. 'Knapwater' describes the actual setting of the house, 'on a hill beside the river'. The Maurward estates belonged to the Grey family who lived originally in the old Tudor manor we pass later in the walk. They built this much larger house as a wedding present for their daughter Lora. It was finished at the close of the eighteenth century and cost the family about £15,000. Tradition has it that George III regretted it was 'built of b-b-brick' and the owner went bankrupt having it faced with stone! In his novel *The Hand of Ethelberta* Hardy makes use of this story. The owner of 'Enkworth Court' (Encombe House), is rumoured to have refaced the house to suit royal taste. Now the mansion forms part of the Dorset College of Agriculture.

Keep straight on past some farm buildings over on your right, through metal gates down the lane to a minor road. Turn left and there stands the old Tudor manor, built of soft grey stone and, as was the custom, in the form of a letter E. Unpretentious and lovely with its tall mullioned windows, it has been carefully restored by Mr R. S. Sturdy. Over the porchway is carved the coat of arms of the Grey family. This is the ruined manor in *Desperate Remedies*. Hardy's critics found it hard to believe two manors could exist so close together. But, of course, Hardy was drawing from life, often stranger than fiction!

Our way curves left round the old manor. Here, below the old house, the Frome runs shaded by great sycamores, half choked by mats of flowers and rushes. Black moorhens, with

One of Hardy's favourite walks followed this track between Stinsford Church and the bridge at Lower Bockhampton. It is the 'embowered path beside the Frome' taken by the carol singers in Under the Greenwood Tree.

Our way curves left round the old manor. Here, below the old house, the Frome runs shaded by great sycamores, half choked by mats of flowers and rushes. Black moorhens, with their vivid orange beaks, dart busily in and out of the reeds, their heads jerking backwards and forwards as if on the end of a piece of string. Follow the path past the walled gardens to the village, Lower Bockhampton. Just before you come to the village street, you will see, on your left, the old schoolhouse, still with its bell over the porch. This was Hardy's first school where he excelled at arithmetic and geography. When the school was opened, Hardy was the first child to arrive and stood waiting in the porch for the other scholars, feeling embarrassed and miserable. And it is Mellstock school in

The Old Manor, Kingston Maurward, the home of Manston in Desperate Remedies.

Under the Greenwood Tree, the home of the enticing Miss Fancy Day. On the night of the carol singing, young Dick Dewy is missed. He is discovered leaning against a tree gazing at Fancy's window. 'A lost man' they all agree.

Turn right to walk down the village to the small stone bridge over the Frome. Cross the bridge, then turn immediately right to follow the beautiful raised path beside the river. This was one of Hardy's favourite paths. He is still remembered walking along here as he did regularly to visit his parents' graves in Stinsford churchyard. In *Under the Greenwood Tree* the carol singers make their way along here too, hurrying down what Hardy called 'the embowered path beside the Frome.' When the path divides follow the main track, right, to Stinsford church. (The other way leads to Grey's bridge.) Apart from worshipping here and playing in the quire, the Hardy family helped to restore this thirteenth-century church. Hardy himself loved this quiet spot and cherished the stories his parents told him about the folk who were buried here and he celebrates them in his novels and his poetry, rich and poor alike. All human life interested Hardy: from the daughter of the Earl of Ilchester who lived at Stinsford House before she eloped with an Irish actor and asked Hardy's father to make their vault in the church 'just big enough for the two of us' to the company in *Friends Beyond*, 'Farmer Ledlow late at plough, Robert's kin, and John's and Ned's ...'

Inside the church gate are the graves of the Hardy family. Hardy's heart is buried in the grave of his first wife, Emma. Close by is the grave of C. Day Lewis, a lifelong admirer of Hardy's work. The gallery in front of the tower, projecting over the nave – where the quire had their victuals and drop to drink during their round of carol singing – has been restored. A plan of the original gallery, drawn by Hardy, hangs inside the tower. As a child Hardy recalls sitting in the church beneath a tablet commemorating the Grey family, among them a certain Angel Grey whose name he gives to one of his characters in *Tess of the d'Urbervilles*. Hardy's own memorial is a stained glass window in the south aisle showing the prophet Elijah.

Leave the church by the main gate. The vicarage, where the Mellstock quire went to talk to Parson Maybold, stands on the right. Turn right, and retrace your steps to follow the path beside the Frome. Turn left along the minor road over the bridge and walk up the street between the cottages. Hollyhocks look in at bedroom windows amid a pervading scent of meadowsweet and honeysuckle.

Opposite the Yalbury restaurant on the left, you pass the old village pump, complete with its handle and stone trough beneath. Walk on from the village to the crossroads. Cuckoo Lane is directly ahead and you can continue along it to the lane on the right leading to Hardy's cottage. But a more interesting route is to turn right at the crossroads, along the road to Tincleton. In just over a half a mile you come to a crosstrack. Turn left along the trck signed for Thorncombe Wood which passes Pine Lodge Farm then leads gradually

Lower Bockhampton village and bridge from the path beside the Frome. The village features as 'Lower Mellstock' in Under the Greenwood Tree. *The carol singers receive no encouragement from Farmer Shiner whose house can be seen (far left) facing the river.*

uphill toward the now tree-covered slopes of 'Egdon Heath'. After a short distance you reach the edge of Thorncombe Wood. Go over a stile to a crosspath. Turn left here along a lovely path running along the edge of the wood with beautiful views of rolling downland on your left. The path winds right downhill, through a gap in a fence to meet a very clearly defined wide way. This is part of the Roman Road which runs west from Dorchester through Thorncombe Wood. Turn left along the Roman Road. It is said that the ghostly figure of a Roman centurion haunts this spot, standing a foot or so above the present level of the ground! When you come to a picnic area turn right and walk along the edge of the wood the short distance back to the car park.

Hardy's cottage at Higher Bockhampton is owned by the National Trust. The house is open 11 am to 5 pm (or dusk if earlier), Sunday to Thursday from 2nd April to 31st October, (open Good Friday). Tel: 01305 262366.

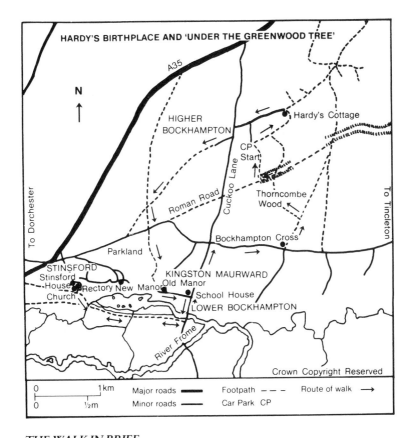

HARDY'S BIRTHPLACE AND 'UNDER THE GREENWOOD TREE'

Crown Copyright Reserved

| 0 | 1 km | Major roads ▬▬ | Footpath – – – | Route of walk → |
| 0 | ½m | Minor roads ▬ | Car Park CP | |

THE WALK IN BRIEF

Distance: five miles easy walking. Allow a full day to include a visit to Hardy's cottage.

From the car park, follow sign uphill through Thorncombe Wood to Hardy's cottage. Turn left past the cottage and down Bockhampton Lane to minor road. Walk left along minor road for a few yards, then turn right down a farm track. When the track bends right, keep on straight ahead through a field gate. Cross the field, hedge close on right. From the next gate keep straight on, across the middle of the field to opposite hedge. The path leads downhill to a farm track. Turn left to minor road. Cross road and follow sign over Kingston Maurward Park. Go through a gate to minor road (farm on right), turn left past old manor, and straight on past walled garden to village, Lower Bockhampton. Turn right down village to cross bridge over Frome. Turn immediately right along riverside path. Path divides, bear right for Stinsford Church. Retrace steps along Frome to Bockhampton Bridge. Turn left, walk through village to crossroads. Turn right for Tincleton. In just over half a mile, turn left up track, farm on left. At edge of Thorncombe Wood, turn left. Keep to this path which bears right, downhill, through a gap in fence to meet wide way. (Roman Road). Turn left to picnic area then right to walk along edge of wood to car park.

2

Puddletown and 'Far from the Madding Crowd'

Walk distance: about 6 miles

On a wet December day in 1872 a labourer was walking down Bockhampton Lane towards Hardy's cottage. He picked up a letter lying in the mud and seeing that it was addressed to Thomas Hardy, he delivered it. The school-children, to whom the letter had been entrusted in the village, had evidently dropped it. So, by a lucky chance, *Far from the Madding Crowd* came to be written. The letter was a request from Leslie Stephen, editor of the influential *Cornhill* magazine, asking Hardy to write a serial. Stephen had read *Under the Greenwood Tree*, he thought 'the descriptions admirable' and added that it was a long time since a new writer had given him so much pleasure.

With such encouragement, Hardy made a momentous decision. Seeing life as he did, 'mainly as an emotion', archi-tecture as a career held little appeal for him. He decided to stay at Bockhampton as a novelist. He wrote to Stephen that he was considering a pastoral tale 'and that the chief characters would probably be a young woman farmer, a shepherd and a sergeant of cavalry'. Again, he chose to write about the people living close to him in the quiet Dorset valleys. Often he walked to places he wanted to describe in his story and recorded his thoughts on the spot. When he carried a notebook he said his mind was 'barren as the Sahara' so instead he used pieces of stone or slate, woodchips or even large dead leaves! He was concerned, as he writes in his Preface, that he should preserve 'a fairly true record of a

vanishing life' so his characters are as realistic as their background. Looking back to the 1840s, he portrays a close-knit
village community within which even the wealthy are bound
by law and custom and the lives of all are adapted to the
seasons with their appropriate agricultural demands. But
modern ideas are threatening accepted views, conflict and
passion can rage as fiercely in a remote farmhouse as they can
in a city street. Keenly aware of these undercurrents, Hardy
tells a fascinating story.

The novel is set in and around 'Weatherbury' – Hardy's name
for Puddletown, a quiet village about six miles east of
Dorchester. We can walk there today, deep into the countryside
and see the background of the novel come alive. Turn for
Puddletown off the A35. Turn left into the High Street
(following large sign for Athelhampton House) and take the
next road on the left signed 'To the Church'. Bear right to the
church where there is room to park. The street to the north of
the church is called The Square. Hardy wrote about the
Puddletown he knew as a boy when he frequently walked over
the heath from Bockhampton to visit his relatives, the Sparks
family. A great deal of the village was rebuilt in the 1860s when
the rows of cob and thatch dwellings were replaced by the stone
cottages we see today. But some old houses remain beneath their
deep-thatched eaves. Facing The Square, once larger and
grassed for grazing animals, is a fine Tudor building. The old
roundhouse, its curved bay supported by slender pillars, also
stands in its original position. Close by, in the Weatherbury Tea
Rooms, we heard that the large house opposite had been the
master's house and that this was revealed only recently when
some papers were discovered hidden in the thatch of the roof.

Ilsington manor stands behind the vicarage, very close to
the church. Until recent times all village life was dominated
by the Lord of the Manor, strictly regulating church and
school. During the hungry 1840s, the time of the novel, life
for the labourers in their often overcrowded, disease-ridden
cottages was becoming increasingly harsh. What indepen-
dence some may once have enjoyed was being eroded by the

St Mary's Church, Puddletown. In Far from the Madding Crowd, *Troy spent a miserable night in this porch after planting flowers on Fanny's grave. His efforts were fruitless as they were all washed away by the jet of water gushing from a gargoyle. The water is now safely diverted into a pipe.*

refusal of landlords to renew leases. When workers were made redundant by increased use of machinery and a reduction in arable farming, it was more economic to pull their cottages down.

One means of forgetting, for a short time at least, insecurity of tenure and meagre wages was drink. So arose what Hardy called 'that love of fuddling to which the village at one time was notoriously prone'. The scene no doubt of much fuddling, Warrens Malthouse, has gone, but some of the paths Hardy's characters trod to it, by the mill and along the streamside, remain the same today.

Puddletown's glory is its beautiful church. From The Square, go in through the north porch. In the novel, Troy, the dashing 'sergeant of cavalry' spends a miserable night here after planting flowers on the grave of Fanny Robin, a village girl he has seduced. Inside the church is a magnificent oak gallery dated 1635. In the summer of 1927, the year before he died, Hardy brought his friend Gustav Holst here. You can imagine them sitting in the gallery beneath the finely timbered roof as Hardy recalls for his friend tales of his father and grandfather walking over from Stinsford, violins under their arms, to help the Puddletown musicians. In *Far from the Madding Crowd* the singers include the shepherd, Gabriel Oak, whose sterling qualities are not appreciated by his employer, a woman-farmer Bathsheba Everdene, until he tells her he intends to emigrate. Another of Bathsheba's workfolk, Henery Fray, a character with a permanent chip on his shoulder, is recalled inside one of the box pews under the gallery. 'Henery', with its extra 'e' is carved clearly into the wood. There is much else to see in this marvellous church,

◀ *Interior view of St Mary's Church, Puddletown showing part of the beautiful seventeenth century musicians' gallery. The Hardy family often walked over the heath and there are dramatic scenes within and around the church in* Far from the Madding Crowd. *Look inside the box pew on the left at the foot of the steps to see 'Henery' carved with its extra 'e', a detail which prompted Hardy to christen one of the workfolk in the novel 'Henery' Fray.*

but I have room to tell only a little of its story. Walk round the outside of the tower and you can see the monstrous gargoyles at the edges of the parapet that Hardy describes in the novel: 'A beholder was convinced that nothing on earth could be more hideous than those he saw on the north side until he went round to the south.' The one on the north-east corner could well be the spout through which, in the novel, rain water pours to wash the flowers off Fanny's grave. I was told that the spout was indeed a hazard until recent times when the water was deflected safely down a pipe.

From the square in front of the north porch turn down the footpath running to the right of the church, past the church-yard to the main road. When you reach the road, turn right, past the school. Follow the road in the direction of Dorchester. Pass a small estate of new houses, on your left. A few yards past the estate you come to a more open grassy area. On the right-hand side of the road you will see two bridleway signs. Follow the sign for Charminster. This route is a little further but as it traces the top of the downs you will be rewarded by beautiful views. Continue along the track passing the recreation ground on the left, then keep to the tarmac turning left then right to cross the bridge over the motorway. The noise of traffic soon dies away as a green path leads you gently uphill. On either side the country gradually unfolds, each flowing curve of field and downland merging imperceptibly to reach at their highest levels, saucer-shaped hollows darkened with gorse and heather. Scattered patches of woodland repeated the same rounded shapes: patterns which have changed little since Hardy captured them in the pages of his novels. As we climbed the hill, crickets chirped in the hot August sunshine and thistle seeds blew across our path like flurries of unseasonal snow.

Follow this pleasant way past two left turnings. The second turning leads to some farms, once possibly a hamlet, called Troytown. Perhaps Hardy named his irresistible sergeant

Troy after them. The other side of Troytown is reached from the main road where once stood an inn, the Bucks Head. Here Joseph Poorgrass, a saintly soul and one of the most entertaining of all Hardy's rustic characters, forgets his duties in a drink or two and develops one of his many afflictions, his 'multiplying eye'.

About fifty yards past the second turning go through a gate. At this point another bridleway runs diagonally across our path. Turn right along the greenway signed 'Druce' leading downhill into the Puddle valley. This valley is the setting for all the country scenes in *Far from the Madding Crowd*. Hardy paints scenes throughout the year, lambing, haymaking, sheep washing and shearing, harvesting, and seasonal festivities. You can see the actual farms around which Hardy based all these events. Druce Farm on the right was the original of the home of Farmer Boldwood, another of Bathsheba's suitors. The bridleway brings us down to the B3142 which runs along the valley. Turn left, cross the road, and look across the field on your right towards the stream.

This meadow, with the small stream running through it, was the setting of the sheep-washing scene in *Far from the Madding Crowd*. When I first came this way fifteen years ago, you could see the remains of the sheep-washing pool with the brick arch which supported the sluice gate clearly visible from the road. It was then just as Hardy describes it in the novel: 'a perfectly circular basin of brickwork in the meadows, full of clearest water...a glistening Cyclops eye in a green face'. The pool has gone but the setting remains the same, and it is not difficult to imagine the scene in this meadow when the sheep are being dipped 'where just now every flower that was a buttercup was a daisy'.

Continue along the B3142 towards Lower Waterston. Some gnarled and twisted apple trees grouped picturesquely on a slope beyond the pool reminded me of the apple gardens which were once such a feature of Dorset. Every farmer and most cottagers – including Hardy's father – owned several of

Old houses beside the Square in Puddletown – the 'Weatherbury'
of Far from the Madding Crowd.

these small orchards. In spring the valleys were pink and
white with their blossom and in autumn the grass was
covered with their small wrinkled apples so good for cider
making. Hardy knew the names of every kind and which
combination of varieties produced the best cider. He helped
his father with the cider making and never forgot the rich
smell of the apple juice oozing from under the press.

Pass the cottages at Lower Waterston and you come to the
venerable manor Hardy immortalised as Bathsheba's home.
He often visited the house and knew, with the trained eye of
an architect, every detail of its heavy Jacobean construction,
its decorative balconies, pillars and archways. Although, for
the purposes of the novel, Hardy writes in the Preface that
'the heroine's fine old Jacobean house would be found to
have taken a witch's ride of a mile or more from its actual
position' he continues that he has not changed its appear-

ance: 'its features are described as they still show themselves to the sun and moonlight'. In the story he describes the manor: 'fluted pilasters worked from the solid stone decorated its front, and above the roof the chimneys were panelled or columnar, some coped gables with finials and like features still retaining traces of their Gothic extraction'. We pass the south front which faces the road and has the original main entrance, an unassuming square porch and heavy oak door surmounted by a cylindrical bow above which rise tall mullioned and transomed windows. From one of these Bathsheba inquired for news of Fanny Robin from her workfolk. The morning after his marriage to Bathsheba, Troy leans negligently out to toss a coin to Gabriel Oak who is passing by with his friend Jan Coggan, and comments that the old place needs modernising. Fortunately, he never gets round to it!

One of the finest scenes in the story is the supper which Bathsheba gives for her workfolk after the sheep-shearing. 'For the shearing supper a long table was placed on the grass plot beside the house, the end of the table being thrust over the sill of the wide parlour window and a foot or two into the room.' As they eat, drink and sing old ballads, night closes in around them 'the shearers' lower parts become steeped in embrowning twilight whilst their heads and shoulders were still enjoying day . . . sat and talked on and grew as merry as the Gods in Homer's heaven'. Hard their lives undoubtedly were, but they possessed a sense of leisure incompatible with life today. The old house stands as a witness.

From the manor, continue along the road for about 100 yards to a track leading uphill on the left. This path takes us back to the ridgeway we left earlier. Turn left and climb uphill past some old horse-drawn caravans, reminiscent of Gabriel Oak's lambing hut. At first a beautiful avenue of chestnut trees borders the track on the left. As the way steepens we bear right through a gate. Continue uphill with the hedge (later a fence) on your left. At the top of the hill, turn left along our former track which you follow for part of the way back. This wide greenway is being used to tend and care for sheep as it was when Gabriel Oak carried his wattle fences over the fields to make shelters for his lambing ewes. Similar fences are still evidently in everyday use, and I noticed a cage, the right size to hold a sheep, attached to a weighing device. Close by was a narrow pen through which the sheep could be driven. After a left bend, look left through a wide gap in the trees for a perfect view of Waterston Manor against a backdrop of arching downland.

When you reach the point on the ridgeway where you previously turned to descend into the Puddle valley, look for a gate on your right. Go through the gate following the sign for Yellowham Wood along a wide footpath running between hedges, and shaded by old oaks and chestnuts. It climbs a little then plunges downhill deep into the wood. Here, Joseph Poorgrass, out at night alone and possibly suffering from his 'multiplying eye', cried out 'Man-a-lost'. Then, an owl happening to cry 'Whoo-whoo-whoo', he answered 'Joseph Poorgrass of Weatherbury, sir!' At the

One of Helen Patterson's original illustrations for Far from the Madding Crowd, *first printed in the Cornhill Magazine.*

bottom of the hill stands a keeper's cottage, the model for Keeper Day's home in *Under the Greenwood Tree*. One of the great trees close by could well be the greenwood tree itself where the guests danced at Dick and Fancy's wedding. We join a tarmac track which takes us to the old main road, the A35. Turn right, with the present A35 running parallel along the embankment on the left. Follow this now peaceful road and turn left to cross the bridge over the A35. Bear left, but before you reach the main road you will see two footpath signs on the right. Turn right to cross the stile into Yellowham wood, Hardy's Yalbury wood. Yalbury wood, so near his home, features in many of his novels and short stories. The route of the old road used to run almost parallel with the A35 uphill through the wood. It is here that Hardy, in *Far from the Madding Crowd*, places the sad meeting between Troy and Fanny Robin as, weak and ill, she struggles bravely towards the workhouse in Casterbridge.

Follow the woodland path straight ahead uphill, ignoring all side turnings. The path bears a little right then descends to meet a track by the side of Hardy's Cottage. Turn left – leaving the Cottage on your right – following the sign for Puddletown. The track climbs the heath which was a wild and lonely place in Hardy's day. Continue over all crosspaths keeping straight on uphill. After crossing a gravel track, the path runs down beside Beacon Hill along what is known as Tolpuddle Hollow. This lovely way, carved through groves of pines, sinks deep into the ground, its sides forming natural gardens of ferns and wild flowers. Leave the wood at the top of White Hill, above Puddletown. Follow the quiet road the mile to the village, descending an avenue of silver grey beeches. Just after a joining road on the right, our road forks. Take the left hand fork and when you reach the main road you will see the lane to the church immediately opposite.

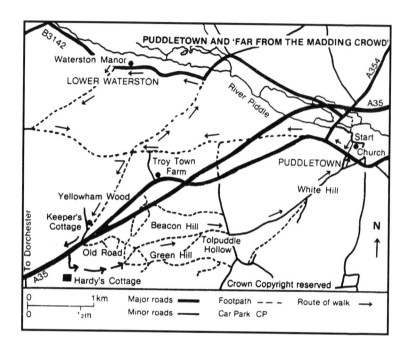

THE WALK IN BRIEF
Distance: about 6 miles. Allow a full day.

From Puddletown church walk down footpath to right of church to road.
Turn right along road past new estate. Follow bridleway sign to
Charminster over motorway. When the way is crossed by another
bridleway, turn right, downhill to Puddle valley, to B3142. Turn left,
through Lower Waterston, past manor. 100 yds from manor turn left along
track. Path bears right through a gate onto the downs then climbs to top of
ridgeway. Turn left and walk to point where you originally left the track to
descend into the Puddle valley. Go through gate on right, along footpath
and down through Yellowham Wood to meet former A35. Turn right and
continue to bridge over present A35. Cross bridge, bear left then right into
wood following footpath sign. Turn left by Hardy's Cottage and continue
straight ahead up the heath to cross gravel track. Continue down Tolpuddle
Hollow to leave wood at top of White Hill, above Puddletown. Walk mile
to village, left at first fork, cross road and follow lane to church.

3

'Egdon Heath' and 'The Return of the Native'

Walk distance: about 7 miles

When he looked out of his bedroom window, Hardy saw in front of him meadows and farmland. These became the world of *Far from the Madding Crowd*. But if he went into the garden and looked the other way, over the house roof to the north-east he saw another, quite different world: a wild, rolling upland, dotted with heath and gorse, scored with strange pits full of holly and rowans, empty except for the wild ponies and an occasional furze cutter. This brooding, rather sombre landscape assumed an almost supernatural character in Hardy's mind as he grew up in its shadow. The heath became symbolic of the fate of man, merciless and unrelenting, and of man himself, slighted but enduring. Hardy expresses these ideas in one of his most powerful novels, *The Return of the Native*. He combines the scattering of wild heaths in this part of Dorset into one great landscape – his immortal 'Egdon Heath'.

This walk explores part of Egdon Heath, just to the north of Hardy's home. We can still see many of the features of the heath he draws upon in the novel. These include the possible site of 'Mistover Knap' where Eustacia Vye lived, the pond close by where she meets her straying lover, Wildeve, 'Blooms End' valley running south from the heath down to the Frome, and the mighty Rainbarrow itself, a beacon hill and old British burial place. The character of the heath has been greatly changed by the pine woods which now cover a great deal of it. However, we shall be walking where it is still possible to imagine its original wildness and capture the atmosphere of this exciting and mysterious world as Hardy knew it.

The walk, about seven miles round, starts from Puddletown church. Park in The Square, and walk along the footpath beside the church (church on your left) to the main road. Cross the road and turning left, continue down the High Street for a few yards until you come to the thatched cottages on the corner of New Street. Turn right up New Steet towards White Hill. In spite of its name New Street is one of the oldest roads in Puddletown. Once each side was lined with cob and thatch cottages. Some of these remain with their tiny windows, thick walls and deep eaves. Where another road joins from the left, keep straight on up the hill beneath a canopy of beeches, their silver-grey trunks overlaid with a soft green bloom. At the top, the edge of a pine wood lies ahead. This was once the open heath but is now part of Puddletown Forest. The bridleway which joins the road on the left is the return route to Puddletown. Follow the road until it bears left round the trees.

The way is now straight ahead, following the bridleway sign to Higher Bockhampton. Hardy would recognise the oaks and beeches of Stafford Copse to the right, but he would be surprised to see the tall ranks of pines climbing over his heath to the left. As we walked along this sunken woodland track early in September, the oaks and beeches were showing their first gold-brown leaves. Faint gleams of sunshine lit the creepers; long coils of honeysuckle and feathery clematis were draped over hawthorns bright with scarlet berries.

Follow the track for about a quarter of a mile. Keep to the track as it runs along the hillside and bears a little left. Soon you will see a wide gravel path leading uphill on the left. Turn left and follow this as it climbs bearing a little right through the pines. When I first came this way, tall pine trees covered nearly all the hillside but many have now been felled. New ones have been planted however so the forests will soon return. On either side of the path you will see those mysterious round hollows scooped out

The view from Rainbarrow on 'Egdon Heath' looking south over the fertile pastures of the Frome Valley.

of the earth which so fascinated Hardy. In one of these, buried among the ferns, he had lain as a child and contemplated the problem of growing up. His conclusion, that he would really prefer not to make the effort, horrified his mother. One hollow, edged with old tree stumps bearing colonies of brown fungi and dotted with dank red and yellow toadstools, reminded me of the ghastly place into which Bathsheba stumbled after Troy had renounced her. As the path begins to level out we meet a joining path on the left. We keep straight on here but first look over to the left to see Green Hill pond. It lies deep in an almost perfect circle of high earth banks, partly obscured by thorn trees set around its edges. If you imagine this pond at the summit of Green Hill without the pine trees, you have the place where Eustacia Vye awaited Wildeve's signal – a stone thrown into the water. And the high embankment could well be where she lit her bonfires to summon him from the valley below. It is probably around this area that Hardy imagined Eustacia's home, Mistover Knap. Hardy used 'knap' as a hill top and this must have been a wild and bleak place in his time.

Here Eustacia stood, looking down at the Quiet Woman Inn where Wildeve lived. Apart from a protecting bank, her home at Mistover Knap stood in the open 'commanding the whole length of the valley which reached to the river behind Wildeve's house'. It is a remote hilltop still and we can readily sympathise with Eustacia, young, passionate and beautiful, when she cries 'do I desire unreasonably much in wanting what is called life – music, poetry, passion, war, and all the beating and pulsing that is going on in the great arteries of the world?'

Keep straight on, leaving the pond on your left. After about fifty yards a road crosses our path. Bear right along the road and follow it as it turns left, past a joining track on the right. A track climbs up the hill to meet the road on the left and immediately opposite you will see a green path bearing right. Turn right and follow this path with the ridge and splendid views on your left. Although it does not seem very obvious at first, this was once the main way over the heath, drained and embanked as you will see, and planted with oaks, beeches and chestnuts to shade the traveller. As you follow it you see how cleverly it keeps its height, unlike the other paths which follow the many shadowy valleys running south from the heath to the Frome. After a short distance, you come to a point where five tracks meet, shaded with chestnuts. Follow the second track on your left, leading west in the direction of Hardy's cottage at the end of Higher Bockhampton Lane. The way is now very beautiful. Tall pines still stand to the left, but on the right the countryside is more open with beech and oak-covered slopes.

When the path forks, bear right. Soon you come to a junction of several paths. Our way takes the second path on the left. But if you would like to visit Hardy's cottage you could make a short detour and turn right here. The path bears left and brings you to the gate behind the cottage. Retrace your steps to the crossroads to continue our walk. Over the crossing track, the way curves past some fine oaks to run south along the edge of the pine forest down its western fringe. Pines now clothe the open heathland stretching away to the right, replacing the thorns, gorse and stunted silver birches that I saw when I first came this way. But it is still possible to imagine the heath as it was in Hardy's time, gold and purple in the late summer sun. Unlike Eustacia in our novel, Clym Yeobright enjoys the sights, sounds and smells of the heath as he cuts furze. Hardy sees Egdon as a predominantly tragic place but he delights in its happier moods as he paints Clym: 'Bees hummed around his ears with an intimate air, and tugged at the heath and furze flowers at his side in such numbers as to weigh them down to the sod. ... Tribes of emerald green grasshoppers leaped over his feet, falling awkwardly on their backs, heads, or hips, like unskilful acrobats, as chance might rule; or engaged themselves in noisy flirtations under the fern-fronds with silent ones of homely hue.'

Pass a track on the left. After about $1/4$ mile the path is crossed by the line of an old Roman Road. As a child, Hardy often walked along this road with his mother and grandmother who told him tales from Wessex folklore as they went. Then, it ran 'like a parting' over the heath. Now, the line is not very clear, but just after a sign for the Roman Road look for a deep wide hollow to the left of the path. The Roman Road crosses just past it. If you are wearing thin soles, you will be able to feel the extra hardness of the road. Thomasin is another person in the novel who feels at home on the heath. She brings her baby 'now of the age when it is a matter of doubt with such characters whether they are intended to walk through the world on their hands or on their feet' to practise taking her first steps on a green place beside the Roman Road.

Now we are coming to the highlight of our walk, the area close to the Rainbarrow which features so prominently in the story. The path to the Rainbarrow and the barrow itself are now overgrown but it is still possible to make your way to it. From the Roman Road continue for about a quarter of a mile until the path starts to descend the hill. After about twenty yards look for a very faint path leading over the bank on the right. The path bears right through the undergrowth for a few yards and on the right a large holly bush marks the site of the largest of the Rainbarrows, ancient tumuli or burial places. However, the fine view over the Frome valley which it affords can be enjoyed without leaving the route of the walk. Do not turn right but continue down the hill for a few yards. The path bears right to reveal the same breathtaking view. Directly below is Duddle Heath, now planted with young pines, which gives way to green meadows each side of the Frome. Beyond the river, low hills merge into a soft haze on the horizon. When Napoleon threatened invasion, the Rainbarrow was one of the famous beacon hills. The materials for a fire were kept ready and the keepers lived in a small earth hut close by, ready to light the beacon when the alarm was given. Hardy describes this in *The Dynasts*.

In *The Return of the Native* the villagers gather here to light a bonfire on 5 November. Eustacia enjoyed this view as she stood on the Rainbarrow looking for Wildeve. Along the valley below runs a minor road from Dorchester, through Tincleton to Wareham. Many of Hardy's characters, like Tess and Angel Clare, travel this road, and look up at the heath, crowned by Rainbarrow. Directly ahead, the cluster of houses beside the road is Norris Mill and further to the south-east, on the edge of the heath, is the site of Wildeve's Inn, the Quiet Woman. Behind, the river shines like a thread of silver and there is a glimpse of the ominous Shadwater weir. Hardy moved the weir much closer to the Inn for the purposes of his story.

Close to Rainbarrow, the persistent sound of the heath add to its wildness. For Hardy, and all in the novel who knew the heath, the particular note in the wind indicated the features of the neighbourhood: 'where the tracts of heather began and ended; where the furze was growing stalky and tall ... in what direction the fir clump lay'. Wildeve, torn with bitter thoughts, hears his own moods in these sounds. 'The pause was filled up by the intonation of a pollard thorn a little way to windward, the breezes filtering through its unyielding twigs as through a strainer. It was as if the night sang dirges with clenched teeth.'

The path plunges steeply down to the valley in the direction of Norris Mill. Keep on downhill ignoring all side tracks. When our track turns left keep straight on up a slight rise then follow it as it drops again to the edge of the cleared woodland. Just before a thin belt of trees follow our main path as it turns left. This is a beautiful walk with trees shading our way on the left and over to our right open views of the valley threaded by the Tincleton road. After Norris Mill the next group of buildings you see beside the road are Duck Dairy. This is where Hardy imagines his Quiet Woman Inn. An Inn called The Travellers Rest did once stand here. Hardy made it the subject of his poem, *Weathers*.

> 'This is the weather the cuckoo likes.
> And so do I;
> When showers betumble the chestnut spikes,
> And nestlings fly:
> And the little brown nightingale bills his best,
> And they sit outside at The Travellers Rest,
> And maids come forth sprig-muslin dressed,
> And citizens dream of the south and west
> And so do I ...'

Look the other way, towards the heath again, and there is the Rainbarrow, dominating the scene, backed by dark pines like battlements. The reddle man, lonely Diggory Venn in our story, looks up from here and sees a solitary figure on the top 'like a spike from a helmet'. It is Eustacia longing to escape from Egdon which for her was a prison.

Follow the green path along the edge of the woodland. Continue past a track on the left. The path bears left to a crossing track. Turn right to meet a minor road to Puddle-town called Rhododendron Drive. Here, Hardy writes, 'the by-road from Mistover joined the highway.' Turn right along the minor road for a few yards in the direction of the Tincleton road. Before you come to that road look for a bridleway leading from Rhododendron Drive on your left. This used to be marked with a bridleway sign 'White Hill $1^1/_2$ miles' but I could see no trace of the sign on my last visit. However, it is a very clear track. Turn left along the track, past some houses on the right. Keep straight on along the woodland path ahead and cross a track to a fork. Take the right-hand path which follows the edge of the wood. This is the direct route to White Hill, above Puddletown and Hardy must have followed it many times. The path climbs gently. Look for a narrow path on your right marked with blue waymarks. At this point we leave our present path (which climbs a little further then turns left). Turn right then immediately left to walk up the side of the field. Ahead you will see two stiles. Cross the one immediately ahead close to the field side. (It has a blue waymark). You are now standing high up on Castle Hill with lovely views in all directions. Our way now drops steeply downhill with the hedge close on the left to cross another waymarked stile. Keep straight on with the hedge on your left to a gate. Our right of way now is straight over the field ahead. Ignore a gate on the left and bear a little right to a gate which opens onto a track. But you may prefer to follow the edge of the field, bearing left then right and right again to bring you to the gate. Go through the gate onto the track which runs left to join the minor road to White Hill and right to 'The Kennels'. Immediately in front of the gate (before the track on your right turns left for 'The Kennels') you will see a small path. Cross the track and follow this footpath through the wood past some houses on the right. Go through a little gate and across the meadows ahead, following the power lines, and you will come out on the road on the corner of White Hill by the bridleway sign we noticed at the beginning of the walk. Turn right and walk down the beech avenue into Puddletown.

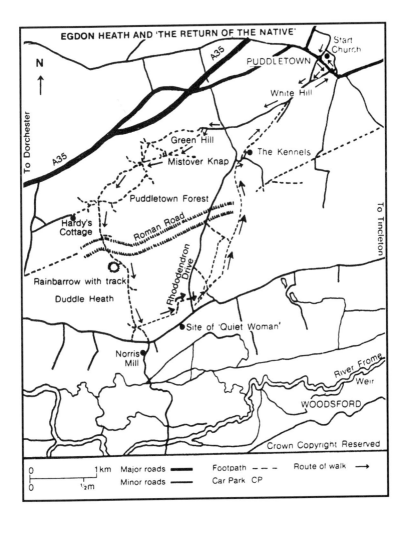

EGDON HEATH AND 'THE RETURN OF THE NATIVE'

THE WALK IN BRIEF *(see previous pages)*
Distance: about seven miles. Allow a day.

From Puddletown church walk down footpath to right of church to road. Cross the road, turn left for a few yards, then right up New Street. Follow road up White Hill to Puddletown Forest. When road bears left, round the forest, keep straight on into wood, following bridleway sign 'to Higher Bockhampton'. After about a quarter of a mile turn left along a wide green path, uphill, bearing right to top of Green Hill or 'Mistover Knap'. When track joins from left keep straight on (pond on left) to meet a road. Turn right and follow road past a joining track on right. The road turns left and a track joins on left. Turn right along the green path and opposite bearing a little right (public right of way). Where five tracks meet, take second left. Go straight over crosstracks (right for Hardy's cottage), the path runs south, down western side of Puddletown Forest. Just after path dips, take narrow track on right to Rainbarrow. Return and follow good track as it bears right steeply downhill. (Ignore track on left.) When the track turns left, keep straight on uphill, then down to a thin belt of trees. Follow our path as it turns left to follow the edge of the woodland with the Tincleton Road over the field on right. This meets a minor road. Turn right for a few yards then before you reach the Tincleton Road, turn left along a bridleway.

Keep straight on to two possible paths. Follow right hand path uphill to narrow path on right. Turn right then immediately left along edge of field. Cross stile and keep straight on to cross another stile. From the top of Castle Hill walk downhill with hedge close on left. Cross stile and keep straight on, hedge on left, to a gate. Walk straight over field (or round it) to gate onto track to 'The Kennels'. Do not follow this track as it turns left for 'The Kennels' but go straight over it and follow footpath to Puddletown. Follow path past houses, through a small gate, across meadows (power lines mark the route) to meet minor road at White Hill above Puddletown. Turn right downhill to village.

4

Hardy's Lyonesse, the Valency Valley and 'A Pair of Blue Eyes'

Walk distance: about 7 miles

Although most of Hardy's writing is concerned with Dorset and neighbouring counties, he set one of his most moving love stories *A Pair of Blue Eyes* in a beautiful part of the north Cornish coast around the tiny fishing village of Boscastle. The story was inspired by his own experiences because it was here he met and fell in love with a girl with 'nut brown hair, grey eyes, and rose-flush coming and going', Emma Lavinia Gifford. The memory of her, against this Cornish background, also inspired his greatest love poetry. Hardy was fascinated by the romance and beauty of Cornwall, preferring to call it by the poetic name 'Lyonesse'. For him, the coast was almost too magical to be quite real. He wrote in the Preface to the novel 'the place is pre-eminently the region of drama and mystery. The ghostly birds, the pall-like sea, the frothy wind, the eternal soliloquy of the waters, the bloom of dark purple cast that seems to exhale from the shoreward precipices, in themselves lend to the scene an atmosphere like the twilight of a night vision'. Yet Hardy felt Cornwall was part of his literary world, calling it 'off Wessex' on his maps. Emma was his 'West of Wessex girl'.

In her *Recollections* written many years later, Emma recalls how she met Hardy. She was the sister-in-law of the rector of St Juliot church, near Boscastle, and at the time was staying at the rectory. Hardy, then nearly thirty, was working as an architect for Crickmay in Dorchester. St Juliot church was in need of restoration and Hardy was sent to make the

preparatory drawings. He arrived at the rectory on a cold
March evening with the manuscript of a poem protruding
from his pocket. Emma opened the door. This was the first of
several visits during which they explored the Valency valley
and roamed the wild cliff tops above Pentargon Bay. Emma
recalls the scene: 'Scarcely any author and his wife could have
had a much more romantic meeting . . . with a beautiful sea-
coast, and the wild Atlantic ocean rolling in with its magnificent waves and spray, its white gulls and black choughs and
grey puffins, its cliffs and rocks and gorgeous sunsettings . . .'
Today we can walk in their footsteps from Boscastle along
the Valency valley to St Juliot, its church and rectory little
changed, and along the cliffs and see this glorious countryside
as they saw it.

The Valency river flows through a deep wooded cleft to the
sea. Here is Boscastle harbour, a tumble of stone and slate
cottages clustering round the narrow inlet. This walk leads
from the harbour, along the Valency valley to St Juliot, then
over the opposite hillside to Lesnewth, the 'East Endelstow'
of *A Pair of Blue Eyes*. From Lesnewth, a romantic glen
brings us back to the Valency valley. The distance is about
seven miles.

Starting from the bridge over the mouth of the Valency
river in Boscastle Harbour, walk through the village up the
B3263 in the direction of Bude. Just past a large car park on
your right is a path leading right, signposted as a public path.
(If you arrive in Boscastle by car this is the best car park to
use for this walk.) Go through the gate and bear left to walk
over Valency Fields.

Follow this lovely path over the meadows and along the
bank of the Valency stream. The valley narrows and steep
wooded slopes rise abruptly either side so that the streamside
path is heavily shaded by overhanging oaks, hazels and sycamores. As we walked we were accompanied by the chuckle of
the water as it swirled round the rocks and tipped over them
in miniature waterfalls.

Emma recalls walking this way with Hardy. 'Often we

walked to Boscastle Harbour down the beautiful Valency valley where we had to jump over stones and climb over a low wall by rough steps, or get through a narrow pathway, to come out on great wide spaces suddenly, with a sparkling little brook going the same way, in which we once lost a tiny picnic-tumbler and there it is to this day no doubt between two of the boulders.' The path is easier to follow now, but a well-placed seat invites you to stop by a waterfall which could well be the one where they lost the tumbler. Hardy

Boscastle Harbour on the romantic coast of north Cornwall where Hardy walked with his 'west of Wessex' girl, Emma Lavinia Gifford, who became his first wife. Beyond the harbour is Penally Point – oddly reminiscent of the profile of Queen Victoria!

remembers the incident in his poem *Under the Waterfall* when:

> '...down that pass
> My lover and I
> Walked under a sky
> Of blue, with a leaf-wove awning of green...'

In his novel *A Pair of Blue Eyes* Elfride Swancourt, the blue-eyed heroine, brings her lover, Henry Knight, to sit by the waterfall. Overhead, the trees are rich with their autumn colours. 'Most lustrous of all are the beeches graduating from bright rusty red at the extremity of the boughs to a bright yellow at their inner parts; young oaks are still of a neutral green; scotch firs and hollies are nearly blue; whilst occasional dottings of other varieties give maroons and purples of every tinge.'

Our way leads past a footbridge on the right. We return to our present path over this bridge at the end of the walk. For the present, keep straight on past a lonely white-washed cottage with stone steps. In the novel, Widow Jethway lives in a cottage similar to this. Beyond the house, the path climbs through a gate to give a glimpse of the grey tower of St Juliot church on the hill ahead.

Where the path meets and crosses the corner of a lane, keep straight on through the gate, following the public footpath sign to 'St Julietta's church'. The path bears left, uphill. Leave the cottage on your right, and climb up to a small white gate. Through the gate, the path narrows for a short distance and runs along the side of a steep bank above the stream. From the ridge you look across the valley and watch the hills unfold, broken by thickly wooded ravines. Occasionally a solitary farm appears, cradled in a hollow. Through another gate, and across the brow of a field, the path goes straight over a crossways of public footpaths. Continue straight ahead for about one hundred yards and look for a slate stile on your left. Cross the stile and bear right, keeping the hedge close on your right. Climb over a stile and keep on with the hedge on the right. The path becomes distinct as it leads along the edge of the fields. Climb the stile and look for St Juliot church on your left. Cross the stone stile into the churchyard, as Hardy did. The little church stands today on its hilltop in as wild and remote a setting as he pictured it. 'The churchyard was entered on this side by a stone stile, over which having clambered, you remained still on the wild hill, the within not being so divided from the without as to obliterate the sense of open freedom.'

Hardy spent many hours in the church drawing plans for the restoration of the tower and the renewal of rotting woodwork. He regretted that much of the beautiful wood-carving would have to be removed and drew the old bench ends. A copy of this drawing hangs inside the church. He also made a careful drawing of the old chancel screen so that most of the old tracery could be retained. To his horror, he arrived at the church one day to find a new and highly varnished travesty of the old screen standing in its place. In reply to his astonished inquiries the builder replied 'Well, Mr Hardy, I said to myself, I won't stand on a pound or two, while I'm about it, and I'll give 'em a new screen instead of that patched up old thing'!

Many years later, after Emma's death, Hardy returned to St Juliot and placed a memorial to her in the church. As the Rector's sister-in-law she had much to do with the restoration work, apart from her interest in the architect. It was Emma who laid the first stone of Hardy's new tower. Her *Recollections* give a fascinating glimpse of St Juliot village as it was in 1870. 'St Juliot is a romantic spot ... it was sixteen miles from a station then. The belief in witchcraft was carried out in actual practice among the primitive inhabitants. Traditions and strange gossipings were the common talk indulged in by those isolated natives where newspapers rarely penetrated ... where new books rarely came, or strangers.' Emma was obviously lively and intelligent and Hardy portrays a great deal of her nature in his characterisation of Elfride. St Juliot village is 'West Endelstow' in the novel and the rectory where

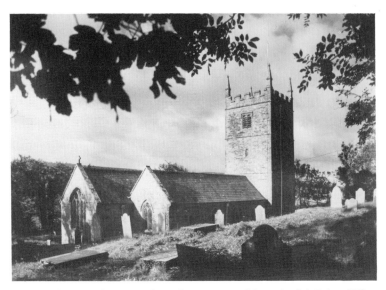

The church at St Juliot, the 'West Endelstow' of A Pair of Blue Eyes.

Elfride lives with her father is very similar to the village rectory where Hardy first met Emma.

From the church walk over the churchyard to the lane running behind it. Turn left (church on your left) and walk up the lane in the direction of the B3263. After a little more than a quarter of a mile a signpost on the right used to indicate our way which is the track running left downhill, to Lesnewth. On my last visit the signpost was missing. If it has not been replaced, look for the track just before a wall letterbox. Turn left down this track and after a few yards the rectory appears on the right.

It was here that Hardy first met Emma. In his notebook he refers to her briefly as a 'young lady in brown'. She was much more explicit in her *Recollections*. 'I was immediately arrested by his familiar appearance, as if I had seen him in a dream – his slightly different accent, his soft voice: also I noticed a blue paper sticking out of his pocket. . . . He had a beard, and a rather shabby greatcoat, and had quite a business appearance . . . the blue paper proved to be the manuscript of a poem, and not a plan of the church, he informed me, to my surprise. . .'. Emma was quickly charmed by this poetical young man from London who shared her delight in Nature.

The rectory is a private home but enough can be seen from the lane to confirm how closely Hardy described this neat stone-built villa, sheltered by its woodland garden, in *A Pair of Blue Eyes*. 'The scene down there was altogether different from that of the hills. A thicket of shrubs and trees enclosed the favoured spot from the wilderness without'. Sitting in the garden, writing the novel, he described what he saw: 'a little paradise of flowers and trees.' Hardy's seat, where he proposed to Emma, is still in the garden. Once they were sitting here, discussing news of the Franco-Prussian War which had been sent to him by his Dorchester friend, Horace Moule, when they noticed a man with an old horse harrowing a field in the valley. Many years later, Hardy recalled this simple scene as the opening of his magnificent poem *In Time of 'The Breaking of Nations'*.

Follow the lane past the rectory as it bears left, then right, downhill to a gate. Go through the gate and straight on with the hedge on your left. Now you cross the path we originally took to St Juliot church. If you would prefer a shorter walk you could turn right here and retrace your route along the Valency valley. For our longer walk keep straight on following the footpath sign to Lesnewth, downhill, still keeping the hedge on your left. The path drops steeply downhill to the water meadows spiked with irises and rushes, either side of the stream. I was delighted to see that a strong new bridge has been built in the place of one destroyed by floods. Cross the bridge and climb the field ahead. The way bears a little left to a gate across a farm track. Go over the stile beside the gate and follow the track which leaves a house on the left and then bears left to join a better track. Follow this which soon becomes a narrow lane, swinging a little left along the other side of the Valency valley. This is a typically Cornish lane: high walls each side draped with ferns and wild flowers and

The Rectory at St Juliot set in its 'little paradise of flowers and trees'. Here Hardy first met Emma, in the porch.

crowned with low, windswept hazels. Hardy liked these lanes 'fenced on each side by a little stone wall, from which gleamed fragments of quartz and blood red marbles...'. Through gaps in the walls are glimpses of St Juliot church on the hillside opposite, but the rectory is hidden amongst its trees. A farmer stopped to talk to us – about Hardy. He pointed out an umbrella-shaped tree on the skyline, above the rectory. His father had told him he'd often seen Hardy sitting there, sometimes writing. Everyone liked Hardy, said our friend, 'he understood country folk'.

After about a quarter of a mile, the lane meets a minor road in Lesnewth village. The old church is immediately opposite. Like many churches dating back to Saxon times, it stands low in a tree-shaded valley. Hardy set some important scenes from *A Pair of Blue Eyes* here in East Endelstow church.

To visit the church, turn right for a few yards and look for a little gate in front of the church on your left. Opposite the porch a footbridge crosses the stream which flows through the churchyard. By the bridge stands a fine Celtic cross. Originally this stood to the west on Waterpit Down. When a curate suggested it should be restored and moved to the churchyard, the farmer on whose land it lay argued he had his eye on it for a pig trough!

In the novel, the mansion of Lord Luxellian stands close by. Hardy imagined the position, borrowing some features of his residence from Llanhydrock House near Bodmin and others from Athelhampton, an Elizabethan manor near Puddletown.

From the church return to the gate opening onto the minor road. Turn left, downhill, along the road to Boscastle. We follow this road for about a mile and a half but it is a beautiful walk. It is one of John Betjeman's favourite lanes. He describes it as 'sylvan'. From the woods the road climbs to give views of the Valency valley, then drops a little through the small hamlet of Treworld. The road dips then climbs again, and in a little over half a mile look for the long grey roof of Minster church half buried in a wooded ravine on the right. Turn right following the footpath sign down the track beside the church. After a few yards turn left to cross a stile and follow the path steeply down to the church porch.

Set deep in its lonely hollow, almost hidden by ivy-coated ashes and sycamores Minster church is the most secluded and peaceful place. Once a priory stood in this narrow glen, but when it was dissolved only the old church remained. Today, it appears by-passed by the busy world, but it is still the mother church of Boscastle. Inside, there is much to see. On the chancel wall is a charming memorial to William Cotton and his wife. Beneath his figure are carved three sons in descending order of height, and beneath hers, five saintly-looking daughters. Outside, there is an unexplained carving of a pair of scissors, half-way up the western face of the tower. To add even more to the magical atmosphere of Minster, there is a holy well in the churchyard.

Climb back to the track again and keep on with the church on your left. After a few yards the track divides. Our way is the left hand, narrow path. Be careful not to miss it. This becomes a clearer path leading you down a steep wooded valley to a footbridge over the Valency river. This is the bridge we passed as we walked down the valley at the beginning of the walk. Turn left and rejoin the original path. Retrace your steps along the streamside walk to Boscastle; a distance of just under a mile. Turn left when you reach the B3262 for the car park and the harbour.

It was dusk as we walked down to the harbour. Boats rocked at anchor and we remembered Hardy's description: 'A star appeared, and another and another. They sparkled amid the yards and rigging of the two coal brigs lying alongside ... the masts rocked sleepily to the infinitesimal flux of the tide, which clucked and gurgled with idle regularity in nooks and holes of the harbour wall ...'. When Hardy returned from Cornwall he wrote one of his sweetest lyrics, *When I set out for Lyonesse*. He concludes that he came back from Lyonesse 'With magic in my eyes!' I think you will too.

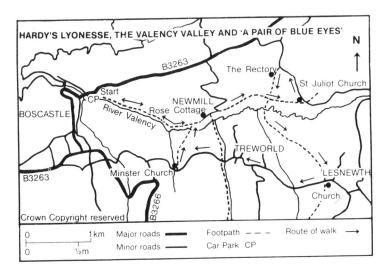

THE WALK IN BRIEF
Distance: about seven miles. Allow a full day.

From bridge over Valency river, Boscastle Harbour, walk short distance up B3263 towards Bude. Just past car park, turn right along public path. Bear left through gate across Valency Fields. Valley narrows, path crosses corner of a lane, keep straight on, through gate, following public footpath sign 'St Julietta's church'. Path bears left past cottage on right and through small gate. Keep straight on, through another gate, over field, over crosstracks. Now turn left over slate stile, then immediately right beside hedge. Follow path over hillside, St Juliot church over slate stile on left. From church walk to lane behind it, turn left (church on left) and walk in direction of B3263. Turn left, following footpath sign to Lesnewth (track just before wall letterbox). Track bends left, then keep straight on through gate and down field ahead. (Meet the original path to St Juliot here. For shorter walk turn right for Boscastle Harbour.) Keep straight on, cross stream, go up field ahead and bear left for farm gate. Cross stile by gate and follow farm track as it bears right past the house then left to meet better track just past the buildings. Follow lane to Lesnewth. At T-junction turn right along the road to Boscastle. (Or left if you visit the church and are standing with your back to it.) Follow road to Minster church. Turn right along path just before the church and walk downhill to rejoin our original path through Valency valley. Turn left to return to Boscastle Harbour.

5

Lyonesse revisited, Pentargon Bay and Beeny Cliff

Walk distance: about 3 miles

After his first eventful visit to St Juliot in March 1870, Hardy returned to Cornwall early in August to supervise the restoration of the church and to renew his friendship with Emma. He found that his 'young lady in brown', well muffled up against the cold winds, had become a 'young lady in blue', more attractive than ever. He frequently visited the rectory and Emma was able to show him more of the Cornish countryside.

The coast around Boscastle is particularly beautiful with its sheer cliffs rising dramatically above the white Atlantic spray and they delighted in its wild loveliness. Emma wrote : 'I showed him some more of the neighbourhood – the cliffs, along the roads, and through the scattered hamlets, sometimes gazing down at the solemn small shores below, where the seals lived, coming out of great deep caverns occasionally . . .'. They went to Tintagel and Hardy was fascinated by the castle, the supposed birthplace of King Arthur. So entranced were they by this romantic spot that they lingered too long and were locked in. They only escaped being imprisoned for the night by much signalling with their handkerchiefs to the cottagers in the valley. It was over forty years later that Hardy made use of his impressions of Tintagel in his play *The Famous Tragedy of the Queen of Cornwall*. In this he tells the rather complicated love story of Tristram and Iseult. Emma records drives to Trebarwith Strand, 'Strangles Beach also, Bossiney, Bude, and other places on the coast. Lovely drives they were, with sea views all along at intervals.'

But their usual walks together were along the coast, close to St Juliot, around the rocky, steep-sided inlet of Pentargon Bay and above the black cliffs of Beeny. What Hardy called their 'wild chasmal beauty' appealed to both of them. The most dramatic scenes in *A Pair of Blue Eyes* are set on these clifftops.

Meanwhile their feelings for each other deepened. Emma wrote: 'We grew much interested in each other. I found him a perfectly new subject of study and delight and he found a 'mine' in me he said.' Time was to sour Hardy's relationship with Emma, but the glory of their first feelings for each other as they walked these cliffs was never lost. Emma died in 1912. Hardy's love for her was revived when he chanced to read her *Recollections* written only a year previously, recalling those romantic days. He revisited Cornwall, and the countryside, particularly around Pentargon and Beeny, brought memories of Emma vividly back to him. He was inspired to write some of his finest poetry. This walk, although it is only a little over three miles in length, takes us to the heart of this wild and beautiful coast.

We start from the bridge spanning the Valency river in Boscastle Harbour. There is good parking either in the National Trust car park just beyond the bridge or in the large park only a few yards away off the B3263 to Bude. From the bridge, walk along the right-hand bank of the Valency stream towards the bay. Go through the National Trust car park and follow the coast path that bears right past the 'Pixies Cottage' towards a row of white cottages on the hillside overlooking the harbour. A splendid view of the tiny harbour – the only natural haven in forty miles of jagged coast between Hartland and Padstow – unfolds below. Once it was a busy port trading its local minerals and slate, china clay and corn for wine and spirits, coal, groceries and bricks. On the long curving jetty, built by Sir Richard Grenville in 1584, stood capstans worked by the carthorses who hauled the slate. The

Beeny Cliff, the 'vast stratification of blackish-grey slate', which features so dramatically in A Pair of Blue Eyes. *Before the cliff, Hardy says, a 'small stream here found its death'. The stream can be seen disappearing over the edge of the cliff in the foreground.*

horses were stabled in the large grey buildings you can see across the harbour, now a youth hostel. The traders needed to be good sailors to negotiate the perilously narrow entrance but in time of war this could be an advantage. A pursued vessel was soon out of sight within the headland and foreign craft who did not know the coast often sailed right past.

The path runs to the left of the row of white cottages. Now the cliffs ahead rise steeply above the gorge-like harbour entrance. To the left is Willapark crowned by the coast-guards' look-out and opposite, the strangely-shaped outline of Penally Point. There is no doubt the shape of the rocks is remarkably similar to the profile of Queen Victoria. We intend turning right before the Point, making for the flagstaff crowning Penally Hill. The coastline ahead dips to form a saddle between the Point and Penally Hill. Just before you come to the saddle a narrow path climbs the cliff on the right. This is our way. The turning is marked by a bright red box containing life-saving equipment. Turn right in front of the box and follow the twisting path to the top of Penally Hill crowned with its flagstaff. When you reach the top the view is breathtaking. Far below on the right, Boscastle Harbour looks like a child's toy dwarfed by towering cliffs and a little beyond it the old village of Boscastle appears, tucked snugly in a hollow beneath the hills. On the left sparkles the open sea breaking and foaming at the foot of the sheer cliffs of Pentargon Bay. There are no paths down these crags and the sea booms deep into vast caverns beneath them. Hardy captures the colours and the sounds of this superb coast in *Beeny Cliff*. The poem begins:

'O the opal and the sapphire of that wandering western
  sea,
And the woman riding high above with bright hair flapping
  free –
The woman whom I loved so, and who loyally loved me.
The pale mews plained below us, and the waves seemed far
  away

In a nether sky, engrossed in saying their ceaseless babbling
    say,
As we laughed light-heartedly aloft on that clear-sunned
    March day . . .'

Follow the path down Penally Hill towards Pentargon Bay,
with the open sea on your left and when the path rises follow
it straight ahead with a wall of vertical slates on your right.
Soon you will see the outline of a large, black cliff face,
overhanging the rocks at its base, forming the opposite side
of the Bay. Even from a distance it looks grim and forbidding.
Opinions differ about which cliff Hardy had in mind as his
'cliff without a name' which features in an exciting scene in
his novel *A Pair of Blue Eyes* but for me this great wall of
rock seems his most likely source of inspiration. The repelling
atmosphere of this cliff suits the action of the novel at the
time. Elfride is walking here with her lover, Henry Knight.
He suggests they should climb over the brow of 'the cliff
without a name'. Elfride agrees although she says, 'I cannot
bear to look at that cliff . . . it has a horrid personality, and
makes me shudder.' In pursuit of his hat, Henry Knight goes
too close to the edge and slips. He is left clinging by his
fingertips from the brink. His position is desperate, '. . . he
could see the vertical face curving round on each side of him
. . . grimness was in every feature and to its very bowels the
inimical shape was desolation.' The cliff is vital to the plot
but Hardy also uses this natural phenomenon in the same
way as he uses 'Egdon' to give tone and depth to his characterisation. Elfride's capacity for loving is shown to be limitless
as she employs all her woman's wit to save Knight. But his is
limited. Like the cliff, he is grand and impressive but unfor-
giving of the smallest slip. He cannot forgive Elfride for a past
incident in her life, unimportant though it turned out to be.
    A stream runs through a shallow valley to the cliff edge and
already you can see the thin thread of a waterfall flowing
from the lip over the vertical rock face. The path climbs to the
top of Pentargon Cliff but be very careful as you follow the

path at this point and do not let small children or dogs run ahead. The cliff edge round part of Pentargon is dangerous and a detour is necessary. Look for a slate stile on your right almost opposite a National Trust sign on your left. You must turn right over this stile as a few yards further on is the crumbling edge of Pentargon Cliff. (This right turn over the stile used to be indicated with a signpost and acorn symbols and I hope these will be replaced.) Cross the stile and turn left with the wall now on your left, a safe barrier between you and the sheer cliff. Bear left to another stile. Cross this and walk on with the wall still on your left. Soon another stile brings you to the other side of the wall again, onto the cliff. Walk carefully now as there is danger of subsidence for some yards. When you reach the highest point of the cliffs above Pentargon the path curves round the headland. Directly ahead is the black face of 'the cliff without a name', part of the Beeny promontory. Between you and Beeny runs the shallow valley with the waterfall. Elfride and Knight walk down this valley on their way to Beeny.

The waterfall between magnificent but rather eerie cliffs was one of the first places Hardy revisited after Emma's death. In *After a Journey* he imagines her leading him back to Pentargon:

> 'I see what you are doing: you are leading me on
> To the spots we knew when we haunted here together,
> The waterfall, above which the mist bow shone
> At the then fair hour in the then fair weather,
> And the cave just under, with a voice still so hollow
> That it seems to call out to me from forty years ago . . .'

The earth wall runs beside you as you walk down the steep hillside to the stream. Now there is a wonderful view of the waterfall, breaking into myriads of sparkling lights over the black rocks. Even from some distance away I could feel the spray on my face.

From the valley, the path climbs steeply up the opposite hillside and round the brow of Beeny cliff. Notices here warn that the cliff edge is unstable so walk carefully if you decide to go further. If you wish you can walk on for a further two miles along this part of the North Cornwall coast path around Beeny. The view was so beautiful that I preferred to stop and watch the sun set over the sea and the birds whirling and calling round the rocks below. The valley was evidently the favourite hunting ground of a buzzard, circling slowly on heavy wings, casting a black shadow over the heather and gorse covered slopes. It is a paradise of wild flowers; when I was there at the end of summer, knapweed, wild mint, field scabious and toadflax covered the hillsides with shades of blue and gold. Peacock butterflies, the 'eyes' on their wingtips a deep glowing blue, poised themselves elegantly on thistle heads and small dusty brown fritillaries drifted ceaselessly around the gorse bushes. A magical place indeed!

Our way back to Boscastle Harbour is by a shorter, inland route, but if you prefer you can, of course, retrace your steps back the same way over the cliffs. For the first quarter of a mile you return by the same path. From the waterfall, climb by the same route to the top of the bay. Look straight ahead and you will see the small grey church of Trevelga on its high cliff above the sea. Hardy may have had the position of Trevelga church in mind when he 'moved' the church at St Juliot to a similar point, close to the sea, in *A Pair of Blue Eyes*. It is interesting that you can guess the possible date of a Cornish church from its siting. Those dating back to Saxon times, like Lesnewth, were built in valleys and hollows to conceal them from marauding Danish invaders. After the Norman conquest, churches could be built in more exposed positions. Headlands were favourite places because the church could then serve as a landmark for sailors.

Follow the path round Pentargon Bay, over two stiles. Now you will see the grey stone stile (which you crossed earlier) over the field ahead. This time do not cross the stile. Turn left and walk down the field, keeping a high wall on your left. Go through the gate directly ahead. This brings you to the B3263 running downhill into Boscastle. You can walk straight down to the harbour – a distance of under half a mile – but I would like to suggest a slightly longer way down a most unusual path. This is a terrace, carved along the hillside above the village, called 'the green cut'.

Turn right and walk down the B3263 in the direction of Boscastle for about two hundred yards. You pass the gates of Penally House and immediately after you will see a white gate on the right. Go through the gate and along the terrace, a wide green way, edged with flints hung with ferns and wild flowers. Now a public right of way to the harbour, it is still called 'the Private Road' because it was created by Colonel Hawker in the second half of the nineteenth century to connect his home, Penally House, with Penally Terrace, the row of white houses on the hill which we passed at the beginning of our walk. After a disagreement with the harbour agent, he made the cut to avoid using the harbour roads. When Boscastle was a busy port the cut was probably noisy with the creaking of carts and the shouts of the carriers. They were trading legally, of course. It is said that smuggled goods were conveyed by a different route along an underground tunnel to Penally House from the sea. So far no one has found the tunnel but Penally House has a ghostly reputation. Unaccountable footsteps have been heard!

The terraced path leads to the row of white cottages, above the harbour. Turn left before the cottages to rejoin the original path. The bridge over the Valency stream, in Boscastle Harbour is a short distance ahead.

THE WALK IN BRIEF
Distance: about three miles.

From the bridge, Boscastle Harbour, walk down right bank of the stream, through National Trust car park, up cliff path to point just below the saddle between Penally Hill and Penally Point. Turn right, up the cliff, by red box of life-saving equipment. Climb to flagstaff on Penally Hill. Follow path on towards Pentargon Bay. Look carefully for a National Trust sign on left and a slate stile on right. Turn right over stile. Bear left to another

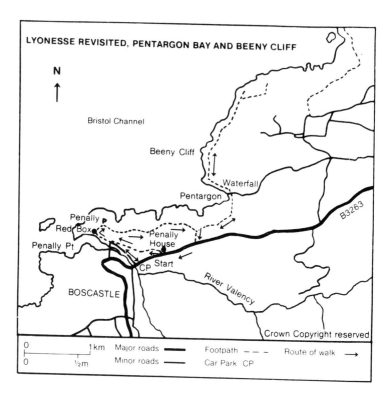

stile. Cross and continue to third stile which rejoins the cliff path further round the bay. Walk down to the valley with the waterfall and up the hillside to Beeny. You can walk further but the cliff edges are unstable. Return by same route, over two stiles. Do not cross the slate stile onto the cliff again, but turn left down field to B3263. Turn right down road for Boscastle, pass Penally House and go through white gate on right. When the road ends at the white cottages above the harbour, turn left along original path for the village.

6

The Purbecks and 'The Hand of Ethelberta'

Walks distances: 5 miles & 4 miles

Thomas Hardy married his 'West of Wessex girl' Emma Lavinia Gifford, in September, 1874, in London at St Peter's Church, Paddington. The success of *Far from the Madding Crowd* made the marriage possible. After a brief tour on the Continent they rented rooms in Surbiton. Hardy could not afford to waste time and when Leslie Stephen asked him for another serial he began work immediately on *The Hand of Ethelberta*. Perhaps because Hardy wanted to demonstrate to his readers that he could handle a variety of themes and settings not necessarily connected with pastoral village life, this was to be a very different novel from *Far from the Madding Crowd*. The loosely-constructed plot rambles from London society – where Hardy never feels confident – to the Dorset coast and the Purbeck hills. The scenes set here in his native Wessex are much more successful than those set in London and contain some of his most lively and dramatic writing. He describes the perilous Old Harry rock near Swanage as standing 'with its detached posts and stumps of white rock, like a skeleton's lower jaw, grinning at British navigation.' And Hardy, the countryman, is never far away. A character is described as 'looking as sick and sorry as a lily with a slug in its stalk'. Touches of his dry humour enliven many scenes. Ethelberta and her party arrive at Cripplegate church to be welcomed by the urbane Neigh. He is 'waiting in the vestibule to receive them, just as if he lived there.' The characters are rather shadowy figures apart from the firm-willed Ethelberta who in her determined bid to provide a

71

Old Harry Rock, 'like a skeleton's lower jaw, grinning at British navigation'.

home for nine brothers and sisters foreshadows the more tragic figure of Tess of the d'Urbervilles.

Hardy also sets an amusing, but at the same time very moving, short story in the Purbecks. *Old Mrs Chundle* is, I believe, a masterpiece. Not a word is wasted as Hardy subtly reveals the characters of the well-meaning young curate with a great deal to learn about people and the old cottager who teaches him the true nature of charity. The story is told with the same light touch and rich humour that we find in *Under the Greenwood Tree*.

Both walks in this chapter start from the car park in Corfe village in the heart of the Purbeck hills. We walk in Hardy's footsteps among breathtaking scenery; along high, smooth-rimmed downs that run parallel with the coast enclosing quiet valleys and through villages built of local stone as much in harmony with their surroundings today as they were when Hardy knew them.

The gateway to Corfe and the Purbeck hills is Wareham, Hardy's 'Anglebury'. The opening scene of *The Hand of Ethelberta* is set here at the 'Red Lion' inn. From Wareham, follow the A351 south in the direction of the romantic ruin of Corfe Castle which dominates the skyline between two long ridges of hills. Drive past the castle ruin and uphill into the village. Look for a car park sign on a wall on the left pointing right, over the road across the square in front of the Inn. Turn right, then follow the sign as it indicates left down a side street. Follow the signs indicating a right turn into the car park. As you leave your car you will have a magnificent view of the ruins of Corfe Castle in sharp outline against the sky. Hardy calls it 'Corvsgate Castle' which seems an appropriate name for this impressive ruin commanding the gap in the Purbeck ridge.

From the car park follow the arrows indicating the one-way system to the exit. (Corfe Castle is on your right). The lane curves to the left to meet the quiet road again. Turn right to follow it uphill between deep-roofed stone cottages standing high on grassy banks. Purbeck stone catches and holds light and every nook and hollow provides a home for flowers. At the top of the hill the lane brings you to the edge of Corfe Common and a little to your left you will see a signpost pointing straight ahead to Kingston. This is 'Little Enkworth' in *The Hand of Ethelberta* and 'Kingscreech' in *Old Mrs Chundle*. Immediately ahead, on the opposite ridge of hills, you will see Kingston village dominated by the larger of two church towers. Our way is directly towards the larger tower. The Common ahead rises a little and then falls to a stream at the foot of Kingston hill. Ignore the signpost pointing down a lane, cross the cattle grid and turn left for about 50 yards. Now turn right and walk downhill to cross a boggy patch by a plank bridge. Now bear a little right as you walk uphill (there is a shallow gully.) From the top you have a clear view of the tower and keeping it directly ahead of you walk down to the other side of the Common marked by a thin belt of trees. Look for a break in the trees and a gate by a footpath sign. Go through the gate and cross the bridges over the stream leading to more stiles. Keep ahead over a small field to another stile and bridge. Bear a little left over the next field. At the other side of the field a post with yellow markings indicates our way. Walk straight ahead over the next field where more helpful yellow waymarks mark our route. Cross a brook and follow a tree-shaded path ahead. This climbs gently uphill through carpets of wild flowers in the direction of the church tower. Cross the stile and keep straight ahead up the field. Cross double stiles and walk up the next field. At the top there is a thin belt of woodland and another stile. The way is not clear at this point, but using the tower as your guide keep straight ahead to the top of the field where a waymarked metal gate leads you into a narrow cobbled lane – just the width of a farm waggon – encircling the hillside below Kingston village. There is little sign of a village as yet, hidden among trees high on the hill. Turn right and walk along the lane for a few yards. Our way is now left but before you turn, look right to see a dense, overgrown avenue of yew trees, still magnificent and sombre. Yews, sacred to the Druids, and the material of the English longbow, are everywhere in Kingston a reminder that this lonely hilltop village is ancient in origin. Turn left and follow a narrow path to stome steps on your right. Climb the steps and walk between cottages and walled gardens that cannot have change since Hardy walked here to emerge in the village street opposite the large church whose tower has led us here.

If you wish to feel the spirit of Hardy's novels when village life was regulated by the seasons and the activities of 'the great house' then pause here in Kingston. It is tiny: just a cluster of cottages and a blaze of gardens both a natural part of the hills which shelter them. In the shop you can buy copies of a book in which Mr Robert E. Dorey, now over ninety, recalls life in the village in times past, *My Memories by a Village Carpenter*. Hardy's works come alive as he describes the great house close by, Encombe. This is

Corfe village from East Hill, looking across Corfe Common towards Kingston on the horizon, far left. Kingston claimed Hardy's old Mrs Chundle as one of its parishioners.

'Enkworth Court' in *The Hand of Ethelberta* – a house which interested Hardy because of its connections with Bockhampton. George Pitt bought the house for his son John early in the eighteenth century. George had married an heiress from Kingston Maurward and Hardy would have recognised his memorial in Stinsford Church. Later Sir John Scott bought the Estate and took the title 'Earl of Eldon'. Mr Dorey writes:

'For village life to go well a leader is always required. Right from the time of the first Earl Encombe provided one. Every aged villager was visited by the Earl or his agent at Christmas, to see that he was provided for, and every employee received a ton of coal. . . . The Third Countess was a charming lady who was loved by all around the Estate for her attention to the needs of the womenfolk.'

Mr Dorey explains why so tiny a village has two churches. The large church opposite the shop, completed in 1880 was, for forty years the private chapel of the Eldon family. Mrs Chundle will have attended the little church you will see up the hill on your left, rebuilt in 1833 by the Earl of Eldon in the place of a twelfth century chapel. Like Stinsford church, writes Mr Dorey, 'The church had a gallery in which a small band of musicians played; both my great-grandfather and grandfather were among them'. Hardy would have enjoyed this shared experience and commiserated with Mr Dorey when he adds: 'When the second Earl and Countess came into the Estate the Countess had an organ installed (so out went Grandfather's cello!)' The Stinsford musicians suffered the same fate.

Today the village street is quiet – almost deserted, but Mr Dorey paints the scene as Hardy knew it, noisy and bustling.

'In my young days it was horses for everything; you knew it was hay-making time when the waggons went by with "ladders" in place. Blacksmith's Shop had three forges going all the time for shoeing horses and making all sorts of ironwork ... Although busy, the village looked lovely. The Earl of Eldon supplied rose trees to every householder, to grow up round the diamond-paned windows. They made a picture for visitors to the village as in the afternoons the housewives stood at their doors, dressed in neat black but with spotless white aprons.'

When the path divides, bear left, again following the footpath sign 'To Hounstout'. The track becomes a pleasant path running along a ridge through woods heavy with the scent of wild garlic. Then you leave the trees to walk along the top of the steep down. Smooth and sheer the hillsides drop at your feet into a beautiful valley opening to the sea. So lovely is this valley that locally it is known as 'The Golden Bowl'. At the seaward end lies Encombe House. It is still as Hardy describes it, a great brick mansion faced with stone, its early Gothic features dwarfed by Classical additions.

In the novel this is the home of Lord Mountclere, the elderly nobleman who plots to win the hand of Ethelberta. The woods to the right could be where Ethelberta wanders to discover the cottage of Mountclere's mistress. Ethelberta's carpenter brother, Sol, looks down on the house as we do and comments 'See, there's the carpenter's shops, the timber yard, and everything, as if it were a little town'. It is interesting that Mr Dorey recalls working in those shops.

Retrace your steps to Kingston village and walk down the village street past the Inn. Keep straight on up the Swanage road for a few yards to the old church. After Lord Eldon's church was established as the village church in 1922, this building became the Village Hall and is now privately owned. You will see remnants of twelfth century carving in the construction. It was here that the new curate persuaded Mrs Chundle, a generous though wily old soul, to attend services. When she pleads deafness he provides her with an ear trumpet, 'she was the centre of observation through the whole morning service. The trumpet, elevated at a high angle, shone and flashed in the sitters' eyes as the chief object in the sacred edifice.' When this is unsuccessful he has a speaking tube installed leading from the pulpit close to his mouth to her ear. Mrs Chundle can now hear perfectly but the unfortunate curate is almost overcome by the smell of her breath. He exclaims, 'What a terrible supper she must have made!'

Immediately past the church on your left you will see a yellow waymarked stile. Cross this, and with the churchyard on your left, walk down to a stone wall. Do not follow the signs past the wall, but turn right before it and keeping the wall on your left walk along the hillside. When you come to a stile, cross, bear a little left then sharply left in the direction of Corfe, keeping a wall and a tiny stream close on your left.

(Ignore a clearer path leading straight ahead). When the main track bears right, keep straight on. Pick your way downhill, still keeping the wall and stream on your left. Cross a stile. Keep straight on with the stream and trees still on your left. Cross a stile and keep heading for Corfe Castle until you come to a gate on your left. Bear left through the gate and follow the path still with the little stream running through trees beside you. The path brings you into the valley to a small wooden gate and stile close to a cottage. Turn left over the stile and cross a bridge to climb the next stile. Turn right to walk round the outside of the cottage garden. After a few yards turn right follwing the yellow signs and walk down to cross a boggy patch of ground over a plank bridge.

You are at the foot of Corfe Common. Cross a narrow stream and keep ahead uphill following the footpath sign for the Purbeck Way and Corfe Castle. As you near the top of the hill, you will see the village and the castle directly ahead. Continue up the grassy hillside to a Purbeck Way marker stone in front of crosspaths. Turn left for a few yards and when the path divides, take the right-hand path to a gate opening onto the minor road from Corfe to Kingston, the B3069. Immediately across the road you will see another gate and Purbeck Way sign. Go through the gate and walk over the Common to another Purbeck Way marker stone. Leave the Purbeck Way here as it turns right and keep straight on for about two hundred yards, then bear a little right uphill to meet a footpath running beside a hedge at the top of the hillside. Follow this path to rejoin the lane end at the approach to the Common. Turn right to retrace your steps to the car park.

Our second walk follows the high down to the right of the castle as you see it from the car park. On the way we can see more of Corfe village and explore the castle. Walk back to the car park entrance and turn left to follow the little street lined with attractive cottages to the square in front of the Greyhound Inn. The entrance to the castle is to the left of the Inn. Like Ethelberta on her way to attend a meeting of the

Imperial Archaeological Association you cross the bridge over the moat and go through an archway into the first ward. Corfe castle must be everyone's idea of a romantic ruin. Slighted by Cromwell's soldiers after Lady Bankes' heroic defence during the Civil War, enough remains of its 'arrow-slits, portcullis grooves, and staircases' to recall its turbulent past. Ethelberta forgot her problems as she wandered alone among its 'windy corridors and mildewed dungeons' before the members of the Association arrived. She had ridden to the castle from Swanage along the down on an ass which she had tied to a projecting stone in the inner ward. We can trace part of her route along this upland path.

From the castle turn left past the Greyhound Inn along the Wareham road and follow it downhill for about fifty yards. (The castle is on your left). On your right you will see a narrow minor road leading under a disused railway bridge. Turn right along this road and follow it along the valley until you come to a gate marked with a blue bridleway sign on your left. Leave the road and follow the path from the gate as it climbs gently up the side of the hill. The terraced path brings you to a gate at the top of the down close to a prominent electricity pylon. Go through the gate and walk on along the spine of the down. We are following 'the lofty ridge' which Ethelberta rode (in the opposite direction of course) and like her we can admire the same wonderful views: north to Poole harbour and south over the valley sheltering Corfe to the final seaward-facing ridge of the Purbecks. Hardy writes: '... the country on each side lay beneath her like a map, domains behind domains, parishes by the score, harbours, fir-woods, and little inland seas mixing curiously together'. Follow the wide green path along the gorse bushes noisy with the scolding of stonechats. Over to the left, above the moors fringing Poole Harbour you hear the plaintive calls of lapwings circling above their very different world. When the way divides, follow the path for Swanage and soon you will see three rounded barrows or burial mounds on your left and a much larger long barrow containing, as Hardy writes, 'human dust from Prehistoric times'. Ethelberta stopped 'on top of a giant's grave in this antique land'. She saw Poole Harbour sunlit. 'Silver sunbeams lighted up a many-armed inland sea which stretched round an island ... amid brilliant crimson heaths wherein white paths and roads occasionally met the eye in dashes and zig-zags like flashes of lightning'. By contrast the valley on the other side was dark and cloudy. 'Here grassed hills rose like knuckles gloved in dark olive ...'. The struggle between the elements suggests to Ethelberta her own conflicting fortunes. Walk on to the other side of Ailwood Down and ahead you will see Swanage, Hardy's 'Knollsea', 'lying snug within two headlands as between a finger and thumb'. Here, the *Life* tells us, Hardy settled with Emma in the July of 1875, to finish *The Hand of Ethelberta*. They lodged 'at the house of an invalided captain of smacks and ketches'. Captain Masters becomes 'Captain Flower' in the novel and Ethelberta rents the same cottage with some of the younger children. The house is West End Cottage off Seymer Road. These downs and cliffs must have reminded Hardy and Emma of their courtship days in Cornwall as they walked daily together. Again, Hardy found inspiration in living in the exact surroundings he describes in the novel. He observes the harbour in all its moods: at its gentlest when 'Breezes the freshest that could blow without verging on keenness flew over the quivering deeps and shallows' to its fiercest in an easterly gale when 'the highest sea prevailed in Knollsea Bay from the slackening of flood-tide to the first hour of ebb. At that time the water outside stood without a current, and ridges and hollows chase each other towards the beach unchecked'. Then the high rocks fringing the bay were at their most terrifying 'the waves leapt up their sides like a pack of hounds'.

From here you can, of course, complete Ethelberta's route and walk on to Swanage. But for the shorter walk retrace your steps along the spine of the down back to Corfe. There are other paths back along the valley but I found I was reluctant to leave the lovely upland and lose my views. Follow the path downhill from the pylon to bear right along the minor road, then left uphill into Corfe and back to your car.

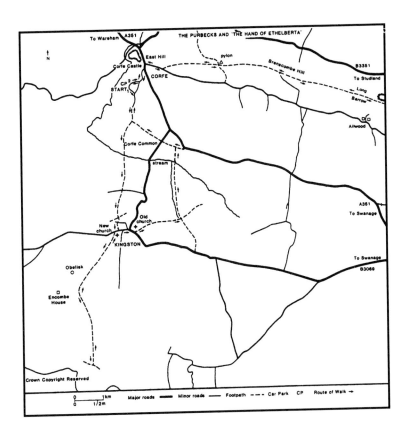

THE WALKS IN BRIEF (see next page)

THE WALKS IN BRIEF *(see previous page)*

Walk one. Distance: about five miles.

From Corfe car park follow signs to exit. Turn right to Corfe Common. Ignore footpath sign. Cross cattle grid, turn left for fifty yards, then right downhill. Walk ahead towards Kingston church tower over Common, cross bridge and stile, bear a little left then straight up fields ahead following yellow waymarks. Go through gate into lane below Kingston village. Turn right for a few yards then left up path. Turn right up steps to Kingston main street. Bear right in front of Victorian church following sign to Encombe. Turn left following sign to Hounstout. Walk along top of down to see Encombe. Retrace steps to village. Walk down village street, past the Inn and straight on up the Swanage road to old church now disused. Past the church, cross stile on left and walk to stone wall. Turn right before the wall and walk along hillside. After stile bear left in the direction of Corfe keeping a small stream on your left. Walk downhill, cross stile and keep on, cross another stile, and continue to gate on left. Go through gate and follow path still with stream on left. Turn left over stile by cottage, cross stile, turn right, then right again to cross planks then bridge to Common. Keep straight ahead up the Common following the Purbeck Way sign to a Purbeck Way marker stone by crosspaths. Turn left for a few yards then, at division, turn right to cross B3069. Continue through gate ahead to another Purbeck Way marker stone. Leave the Purbeck Way here and keep ahead for about two hundred yards then bear a little right uphill to a footpath. Continue to lane end at approach to Common. Turn right and retrace your steps to the car park.

Walk two. Distance: four miles, some gradual climbing.

From Corfe car park return to entrance. Turn left to Square. Bear left to visit Castle. Return to Square and with the Greyhound Inn on your left follow main road downhill in the direction of Wareham. Turn right along narrow road under disused railway bridge. Follow lane to waymarked gate on left. Go through gate and climb path up to top of down by electricity pylon. Keep on along spine of down to gate at far side of Ailwood Down. Retrace steps to Corfe.

7

Sturminster Newton, 'Our Happiest Time'

Walks distances: about 2 miles each

Hardy finished *The Hand of Ethelberta* in January 1876 and sent the manuscript to Leslie Stephen for publication. Still looking for a more permanent home, he and Emma moved into lodgings in Yeovil in March. In May they toured Holland and the Rhine. Returning to Yeovil in June Hardy resumed his search for a home even more diligently having heard relatives remark that he and Emma 'appeared to be wandering about like two tramps'. By midsummer they had found a house where they were to spend their happiest days, built high on a cliff overlooking the river Stour on the outskirts of Sturminster Newton in the Blackmore Vale. After a quick dash to Bristol where they bought a hundred pounds worth of furniture in two hours they moved into Riverside Villa, as the house was called, at the beginning of July.

Visit Sturminster Newton today and you will appreciate the charm that so captivated the Hardys. Its quiet streets are still a fascinating blend of medieval gables, coaching inns and pretty Georgian cottages. Outside the thatched market house are the octagonal steps of a cross where folk from the surrounding countryside have gathered to buy and sell since Saxon times.

A pleasant way to approach Sturminster Newton is to take the A357 from Wimborne through Blandford Forum, following the lush, green valley of the Stour. The rounded, wooded combes so typical of Dorset rise above the fields and as you approach Sturminster you see the bare slopes of great hill forts, Hod Hill and Hambledon Hill, where men lived more than two thousand years ago. Turn right for Sturminster across the beautiful medieval bridge. The tower of the parish church of St Mary dominates the roofs of the little town on the hillside ahead. There is plenty of parking space but the best car park for a long stay is off Station Road. Drive through the Market Place and you will see Station Road on the right. Walk back up the street to the Market Square. In the centre are the worn grey steps of the cross. This was originally the site of Sturminster's famous cattle market which has now been moved to the north of the town, but it is still a busy scene on market days. It was busy when I was there although it was Sunday. Artists were at work on street corners, in doorways, or perched on the steps of the cross, all engaged in capturing the charm of Sturminster's shadowed gables, mossed roof tiles, deep thatch and gracefully curved bow windows. Imagine these narrow streets thronged as they were on Coronation Day, 28 June, 1877, when Hardy wrote this note: 'games and dancing on the green Stewards with white rosettes. One very anxious fearing that while he is attending to the runners the leg of mutton on the pole will go wrong; hence he walks hither and thither with a compressed countenance and eyes far ahead. The pretty girls, just before a dance, stand in inviting positions on the grass'. The Hardys allowed their servant girl to go to Bournemouth for the celebrations. She returned, only to elope that evening with her young man. Later, when the two were married, the Hardys visited them.

Facing the cross with the market house behind it, our way is to the right of the Market Place, then down Ricketts Lane. Turn right down the lane, following the sign to the war memorial and recreation ground. A gate leads to a path running beside a wide green which slopes down to the meadows beside the river. Follow the path along the edge of the green. The last house on your right is Riverside Villa. The house is a grey, semi-detached, typically Victorian villa, but turn right through the gate just beyond it and you will see why the Hardys liked it so much. You are standing on the top of a gently sloping grassy cliff. Beneath you, the Stour edged with water lilies swirls round a willow covered island and vanishes in the distance between tall banks of rushes. Beyond, stretching to the horizon, are meadows and farmlands.

Hardy found this country irresistible. A day or two after their arrival he wrote: 'Rowed on the Stour in the evening, the sun setting up the river. Just afterwards a faint exhalation visible on surface of water as we stirred it with the oars. A fishy smell from the numerous eels and other fish beneath. Mowers salute us. Rowed among the water lilies to gather them. Their long ropy stems. Passing the island drove out a flock of swallows from the bushes and sedge, which had gone there to roost. Gathered meadow sweet . . . .'. They were both delighted the house faced west so they could watch the sun setting over this lovely scene.

They were not alone in this. Hardy wrote: 'A man comes every evening to the cliff in front of our house to see the sun set, timing himself to arrive a few minutes before the descent.' Here, with this countryside before him, Hardy felt at home. He notes with the practical eye of one used to cultivating useful crops that in Sturminster there are few traces of city sophistication: 'Vegetables pass from growing to boiling, fruit from the bushes to the pudding, without a moment's halt, and the gooseberries that were ripening on the twigs at noon are in the tart an hour later.'

At this time, Hardy was too busy enjoying his cliff top home to write about it, but many years later he was to remember these happy days in nostalgic poems. His mind possessed the power to receive and store impressions, often for a very long time, then to record them with a freshness that seems immediate. At Sturminster he wrote *The Return of the Native* in which he gives a vivid picture of his native heath, over twenty miles away.

From Riverside Villa, Hardy could walk down to the Stour by two paths. We shall go down by one and come back along the other. Follow the track from Hardy's home down the hillside and over the stile at the foot. Turn left and cross the meadow towards an iron footbridge with white rails that

The old mill at Sturminster Newton, Hardy's 'Stourside Mill,
where broad Stream lilies throng'.

leads you over the river. This is Colber Bridge, built in 1841.
The stone supports beneath seem much older and as he
looked over the rail Hardy probably saw wild flowers and
hazels growing in their damp crannies as we do today. Hardy
enjoyed long walks along these river banks. In his diary for
30 May, 1877, he records walking to Marnhull: 'The prime
of bird-singing. The thrushes and blackbirds are the most
prominent – pleading earnestly rather than singing and with
such modulation that you seem to see their little tongues curl
inside their bills in their emphasis. A bullfinch sings from a
tree with a metallic sweetness piercing as a fife.' These
impressions were stored in his memory too until they found
expression in his novel *Tess of the d'Urbervilles*. Tess's home
is at Marnhull, or 'Marlott' as Hardy renames it. The careful
notes on birdsong were not wasted. There is a great deal of
bird imagery in the novel.

Cross Colber Bridge. Ignore the yellow footpath sign indicating a path to the right. Bear left following the sign for Stalbridge Lane. Follow this over the meadow ahead to the hedge. As you approach the hedge you will see two iron gates. Aim for the second gate and cross the stile to the right of it to follow the footpath straight ahead which leads to Stalbridge Lane. Turn left along this narrow way, sunk deep between high banks crowned with hazels and honeysuckle. Every now and again there are glimpses of the river as it winds beneath the willows on the left. On the cliff above are the houses of Sturminster with Riverside Villa prominent on its corner. The lane burrows past thatched cottages with their apple gardens full of gnarled and twisted trees, their lower branches lost among the tall grass and ox-eye daisies. Close to the river, teasels raise prickly brown heads among the dragonflies.

After about a third of a mile the river curves closer to the lane by a half-timbered house and the lane rises a little uphill. Now look for a stile on the left. Leave the lane and go over the stile, following the path sloping down to the river and the interesting old mill beside it. Part of this massive stone building with its low timber-framed doorway and wooden gallery dates back to the seventeenth century. When I first visited Sturminster the old mill had fallen out of use, but now it must look very much as it did in Hardy's time. It has been restored and you can look round it – even buy some stone-ground flour if you wish.

The five hatches, weir and millstream are crossed by bridges which take us to the opposite side of the Stour to the meadows below the recreation ground. Go through the wooden gate and with your back to the Mill, look straight ahead over the meadow to a gate. Beyond the gate you will see the green in front of the south wall of Riverside Villa. You are standing where Hardy imagined himself in *The Musical Box*, one of several poems he wrote after Emma's death when he revisited Sturminster in June 1916. He writes:

'I had slowed along
After the torrid hours were done,
Though still the posts and walls and road
Flung back their sense of the hot-faced sun,
And had walked by Stourside Mill, where broad
   Stream lilies throng.
   And I descried
The dusky house that stood apart,
And her, white muslined, waiting there . . .'

Walk up the meadow, through the gate in the direction of Riverside Villa. When you reach the house, pause on the top of the cliff beneath fine beech and chestnut trees to look at the river below. Here Hardy wrote his poem *Overlooking the River Stour*. Fascinated by the birds swooping low over the water, he wrote:

'Like little crossbows animate
The swallows flew in the curves of an eight
Above the river gleam . . .'

To finish our first walk, turn right along the edge of the recreation ground and down Ricketts Lane to turn left for the cross and Market Place.

We begin our second ramble from Sturminster Newton's beautiful fifteenth-century church. Approaching the Market Place from Rickett's Lane turn right opposite the Westminster Bank before you come to the cross. Follow Church Street as it bears right and runs gently down to meet a lane. Turn left and you are facing the west front of the church. Built in the soaring perpendicular style, the church is full of interest. Most lovely is the rounded 'wagon' roof of the nave, decorated with carved wooden angels.

To begin our walk, follow the footpath leading from the north side of the church to the upper end of Penny Street. (From the west front walk along the side of the churchyard, leaving the church on your right. The footpath is on your left.) The large gateway on your right is the entrance to the

The Stour curving through the meadows below Riverside Villa, the home of the Hardys in Sturminster Newton.

old Boys School. The school is built on a massive scale of honey-coloured stone, with heavy gables and mullioned windows. It claims as one of its former pupils Dorset's most loved dialect poet, William Barnes. The son of a local farmer, Barnes attracted the attention of a solicitor, Henry Dashwood, who lived in Vine House. (His house is still there, opposite the school.) He did so in an amusing fashion. Young Barnes, aged twelve, had been sent to clear a field of dung. Instead of getting on with his task, he turned his wheelbarrow on end and began a chalk drawing of a cow on one side of it. Mr Dashwood happened to be passing and was much impressed with the drawing. He called at the school and discovered that the artist was also a clever student. He immediately employed Barnes as a clerk in his office. After work Barnes continued his studies, teaching himself Greek and Latin and seventeen other languages. So hard did he study that by the age of twenty-two he was able to set up his own school. But with his brilliant scholarship Barnes combined a deep love of the countryside and the people he knew who spoke the dialect of the Blackmore Vale. He was nearly sixty when he kept school in Dorchester next to Hick's office where the young Thomas Hardy was studying to become an architect. When Hardy had any problems with his study of Greek he would rush next door to consult Barnes. So a friendship was formed which lasted until Barnes's death.

To look at more of the countryside which both poets loved, turn right down Penny Street, past the huge buttressed walls of the old school. You pass a farmyard on the left. Look for a path leading left immediately after the farmyard, just before Penny Street turns right. Turn left and follow this footpath leading to the meadows beside the Stour, east of the town. As you enter the first meadow bear right along the less clearly defined path. You can continue beside the river to Fiddleford Mill, a distance of just over a mile. I came this way early in July when the river flowed swiftly under the trailing willows. The still water close to the banks was overlaid with white and gold lilies floating serenely above their dinner-plate leaves. On the other side of the river rise thickly wooded hills. These are the fields where Barnes worked as a boy which he remembers in his poem *Leaves of Summer*:

> 'Leaves of the summer, lovely summer's pride,
> Sweet is the shade below your silent tree ...'

Fiddleford Mill is a delight. Part of the house dates from the fourteenth century. The mill-house, sluices and footbridge by the pond can all be visited. Today a more peaceful picture would be hard to imagine, but once rowdy scenes took place here. The mill was well-known as a hiding place for contraband liquor and the factory workers from Sturminster flocked to this secluded spot for a cheap drink. But as you walk back beside William Barnes' 'cloty Stour' I think you are more likely to be reminded of his most famous poem

Rustic Childhood which contains these lines:

> 'I spent in woodland shades my day
> In cheerful work or happy play.
> And slept at night where rustling leaves
> Threw moonlight shadows o'er my eyes.
>   I knew you young and love you now,
>   O shining grass and shady bough.'

Hardy could not fail to appreciate his fine verse and wrote a glowing tribute to his friend as a preface to a collected edition of his poetry.

There is a little more of Sturminster I would like you to see. When you rejoin Penny Street turn left and walk to the church through the area known as Tanyards. Obviously leather tanning must once have taken place here. Past some cob and thatch cottages you come to a wide green churchyard in the middle of which stands a splendid tree rivalling the church tower in height. Across the green, the mellow stone buildings include the old school house. Over the wall on your left is the vicarage overlooking a beautiful sweep of the river. Sixteen people were once employed in the house and grounds and the great bell on the north wall was used to summon the outdoor staff. Turn right down Church Street for the Market Place and the cross.

It is difficult to imagine why the Hardys should wish to leave as delightful a place as Sturminster Newton. But, temporarily at least, Hardy felt that the right atmosphere for an aspiring novelist could only exist in London. So on 18 March, 1878 he wrote in his diary: 'End of Sturminster Newton idyll. . .'. Many years later he was to add 'our happiest time'.

THE WALKS IN BRIEF
Walk one. Distance: about two miles.
From the cross, Sturminster Market Place, turn right down Ricketts Lane for recreation ground. Walk along side of ground to corner by Riverside Villa. Turn right, through gate and down hillside. Left at the foot to Colber

Bridge. *Walk to the hedge, then left along it to second gate on right. Cross stile beside it and follow footpath straight ahead to Stalbridge Lane. Left along the lane for about one third of a mile, to a stile on left. Over stile and down the hill to the Mill. Cross river and walk up the hill to Riverside Villa. Turn right for Ricketts Lane, the Market Place and the cross.*

Walk two. Distance: about two miles.
From Ricketts Lane turn left towards the Market Place. Before the cross, turn right opposite Westminster Bank. Turn right and follow Church Street to lane. Turn left for the church. Turn left from north side of churchyard along footpath past the old school (on right) to Penny Street. Turn right down Penny Street, taking the footpath left for Fiddleford. Take right hand path in first meadow.

Walk by the Stour to Fiddleford Mill. Retrace your steps to Penny Street. Turn left through Tanyards to the church. Look over the wall on the left for a view of the old vicarage. Turn right down Church Street for the Market Place and the cross.

8

Owermoigne and 'The Distracted Preacher'

Walk distance: 4½ miles

In March 1878 the Hardys left Sturminster Newton and moved to London taking The Larches, Arundel Terrace (now 172 Trinity Street) in Upper Tooting near Wandsworth Common, on a three year lease. The following months were busy and exciting. Hardy introduced Emma to scenes like the Lord Mayor's Show which they watched from an upper window in the office of *Good Words* magazine in Ludgate Hill. Emma commented that the crowd reminded her of boiling porridge. They took an active part in London society, meeting among other literary figures, Browning, Tennyson and Matthew Arnold. During this busy time Hardy wrote two of his most delightful and amusing works: *The Distracted Preacher* (a long 'short story' which is almost a novelette) and his only historical novel *The Trumpet Major*.

Both works abound in humour and gentle irony and are set among the seaward facing downs overlooking Weymouth and Portland Roads. Hardy knew this area well and enjoyed its history and folklore which he weaves into his stories. To make certain he captured the feel of the countryside correctly he visited Weymouth in February 1879 and again in August of the same year.

Hardy had been told stories about smuggling days from his boyhood at Bockhampton. The cottage had been used as a 'staging post' by smugglers and *The Distracted Preacher* is loosely based on a series of true incidents. The story takes place in the 1830's when smuggling along the Dorset coast was still a thriving local industry, enjoyed by most of the inhabitants. Small barrels of gin and brandy 'accidentally floated over in the dark from France' as Hardy tells and, he comments, were as well-known to the villagers as turnips. At this time it was still considered a game to outwit the 'preventive men' by a variety of ruses and there was little bloodshed. Times changed however when the law enforcers were granted blood money and both sides took up arms. Hardy uses these changed circumstances to redeem his heroine, Lizzie Newberry, a confirmed smuggler thoroughly enjoying every minute of her 'ventures'. A bewitching widow, living in a large house in 'Nether Moynton' (Hardy's name for Owermoigne) she takes as a lodger Mr Stockdale, the newly-arrived Wesleyan minister, a highly respectable young man from an inland town. He is a doomed man from the moment he sees her and his horror when he discovers her profession is only matched by his increasing devotion to her charms. Lizzie cures his cold with a little spirit drawn from a cask hidden in the church tower and against his will he becomes involved. How he follows Lizzie on her escapades, desperately trying to square his conscience the while, is told with such comic relish that I suspect Hardy was smiling as he wrote. The conventions of magazine writing forced him to end the story with Lizzie's repentance but in May 1912 he added an alternative ending. You must read the story to decide which you prefer!

Today we can still walk in this smugglers' country of downland and cliffs following Lizzie on one of her ventures. We begin our walk at Owermoigne, a small village just off the A352 between Dorchester and Wareham. Park close to the church. Owermoigne is still an attractive village. The church, very much as Hardy describes it in the story, stands beside a green ringed with stone-built thatched cottages. Church registers date from 1596 and they record the baptism of members of the Hardy family who lived in the village from 1664–1793 so Hardy probably had a special reason for choosing Owermoigne as the setting for his story apart from the village's reputation for smuggling. Evidently the squire and the parson were equally involved. When Stockdale joins

Owermoigne Village

the smugglers on top of the church tower, anxiously watch-ing the preventive men searching the village below, Jim Clarke is not pleased to see him. 'If the pa'son should see him a-trespassing here in his tower, 'twould be none the better for we, seeing how 'a do hate chapel-members. He'd never buy a tub of us again, and he's as good a customer as we have got this sode o'Warm'll.' His tub was no doubt passed through the now bricked up window in the cellar of Owermoigne rectory. A small locked door in the tower leads to the spiral staircase to the bell loft and flat roof of the tower that gave the smugglers a refuge and ideal vantage point. They peered through the battlemented top of the tower to watch the searches of the preventive men among the apple trees in Miller Owlett's orchard close by. To the west of the tower a small orchard still exists. Much to the smugglers' chagrin, their barrels were eventually discovered in a brick-lined pit beneath an apple tree which was planted in a box on top of the pit. In his Preface to the story Hardy tells us that this method of concealment was 'precisely as described by an old carrier of tubs – a man who was afterwards in my father's employ for over thirty years'. And it is easy to imagine Lizzie leading Stockdale over the low stone wall at the bottom of her garden across the graveyard into the tower where the 'things' (as the smugglers termed the barrels) were concealed beneath the lumber.

Lizzie's plans for a landing of a consignment from Cherbourg at 'Ringsworth' (Hardy's name for Ringstead Bay) are overheard by the preventive men so she sets off at night 'to burn the lugger off'. Full of misgivings, Stockdale secretly follows her. Our walk follows them. From the church porch turn right towards the little green, leaving the whitewashed thatched cottages on your left. Keep straight on here with the

Owermoigne Church with the orchard where the smuggled tubs were buried just beyond the tower.

green on your right and follow the lane as it bears left towards the main road, the A352. We can imagine Lizzie, dressed in her dead husband's greatcoat and boots, tripping along before us 'at a quickening pace till the lane turned into the turn-pike road, which she crossed, and got into the track for Ringsworth.' Cross the A352 and immediately ahead, climbing rather steeply uphill you will see the track she followed. This is a quiet lane still, and, as indicated, it has no vehicular access to the sea. It is steep but as we are following Lizzie who 'ascended the hill without the least hesitation' so must we. You will be rewarded with lovely views of the curving downlands. The lane dips to pass 'the lonely hamlet of Holworth'. There is a farm on your left opposite a duck-pond and our return route rejoins the lane in front of the farm. The lane now ends to become a bridleway and there is still a gate at this point 'between the downs and the road'. Here the exhausted Stockdale, having lost sight of Lizzie as she rushed home, paused to rest. As you climb the down there is the shimmer of the sea in the distance. Then as you reach the top and descend slightly to a crossing track a magnificent view spreads before you. Across Ringstead Bay lies Portland with its harbour linked to the mainland by the thin arm of Chesil beach. Below you the rough gorse-covered slopes of Burning Cliff tumble to the sea. The cliff takes its name from shale-burning underground, but it is pleasant to suppose that the activities of Lizzie and others like her may have suggested the name. The lugger with the contraband had to be warned not to land its cargo at Ringstead as planned so, having reached the top of the cliff she climbed a conspicuous mound and set alight to a gorse bush. The flames flaring suddenly in the dark made an excellent signal.

Lizzie – with Stockdale in pursuit – rushed back the way she had come but this country is too lovely for us to leave so soon. There are beautiful walks along the crossing track in both directions. These cliffs are owned by the National Trust and are specially rich in flowers and wildlife. To continue our walk turn left along the crossing track for a few yards to where there are two possible paths indicated by a marker stone. Our way is straight on here in the direction of West Lulworth but you may prefer to turn right along the other path and walk the half mile down to the beach. It is a steep climb back and we have to sympathise with the smugglers struggling up with a 'pair of spirit-tubs slung upon the chest and back'. Hardy comments in the Preface that this produced a 'horribly suffocating sensation ... after stumbling with the burden of them for several miles inland over a rough country and in darkness.'

To see some more of the downland country which the smugglers crossed around Chaldon, follow the path to West Lulworth, past a thatched barn on the right, for about a quarter of a mile. At the top of a rise there is a signpost. Turn left through a gate. Follow the bridleway straight on and look carefully for a signpost on the left. At this point our way to West Chaldon is right, over a low bank and across the field as indicated by the signpost. (Be careful not to miss this turn as the path straight ahead is private.) I came this way in May and could see no trace of the path to West Chaldon through the tall grass but I was assured that this was the correct way and later a path would be visible. The way to West Chaldon is indicated at intervals by blue bridleway arrows on small stones and by wooden signposts but the path between them is not clear. So turn right over the bank and keep ahead over the field along the side of the down following the line of the power cables. A little to your left you will see a gap in the hedge and when you reach it a small marker stone. Follow the direction indicated for West Chaldon straight across the next field. Here there is a wooden signpost beside a small iron gate. Bear half-left over the next field as the sign indicates. (Ignore the path ahead leading past the power cables). Continue to a wooden footpath sign and follow a track which bears a little right then left into the small bowl of downland that encloses West Chaldon.

Our path brings us to a lane. Turn left towards West

Burning Cliff above Ringstead Bay where Lizzie warned off the lugger in the story The Distracted Preacher.

Chaldon Farm. Just before the farm look carefully on the left for a footpath sign pointing right, between the farmhouse which you pass on the right and farm buildings which are on the left. Follow this past the farm to a stile. (Our route is now indicated at times with stones waymarked with yellow footpath arrows). The stile pointed a little left in the direction we must follow up the hill. (Ignore an obvious path scored out of the hillside). At the top of the rise you will see a yellow waymarked stile leading into a field on your left. Cross the stile and walk on beside the field with the hedge on your right. Looking back towards West Chaldon you can see the little valley which was the site of a medieval village and the hillside above is terraced to form lynchets. Cross the next stile. Our way is diagonally across the next field but I found the easiest way to find the correct signposted stile was to walk straight across to the hedge on the other side. Turn right, and with the hedge on your left walk down the field close to the hedge, following it as it bears left then right past some houses to a footpath sign and stile on the left. Cross the stile and continue over paddocks and stiles to pass a house on your right. Follow the grassy path ahead to cross more stiles and paddocks to a farm track. Go over the track and through the gate opposite. Blue arrow waymarks indicate the route curving a little left up a field to a farmyard. Bear right past a farmhouse on your right to rejoin the lane we followed earlier opposite the duckpond. Turn right to retrace your steps back to Owermoigne.

THE WALK IN BRIEF
Distance: 4¹/₂ miles. Allow plenty of time to admire the views.

Park near the church in Owermoigne village. From church porch turn right and follow lane as it bears left to main road, A352. Cross to lane ahead and follow it to crossing track above Ringstead Bay. Turn left along crossing track for few yards then go through gate and follow path signed West Lulworth. At the top of rise turn left for West Chaldon. Look for signpost on left pointing right over a low bank for West Chaldon. Cross the field along side of down to next signpost a little to your left. Follow direction indicated over next field. From signpost bear half-left over the field as the sign indicates. Continue to next footpath sign. Follow the direction indicated downhill to West Chaldon. Join lane, turn left. Just before West Chaldon Farm look for footpath sign on left pointing between the farmhouse on right and farm buildings on left. Follow this to a stile and bear left along less obvious path to stile on left. Cross stile and walk with hedge on right. Cross next stile, walk straight on to hedge, turn right and keeping hedge on your left walk down field to footpath sign and stile on left. Cross stile, continue over paddocks and stiles, past house on right to take grassy path leading to more stiles and paddocks and a farm track. Cross track, go through gate opposite and bear a little left up field to a farmyard. Bear right past farm on right to lane. Turn right to retrace your steps to Owermoigne. Distance: 4¹/₂ miles. Allow plenty of time to admire the views.

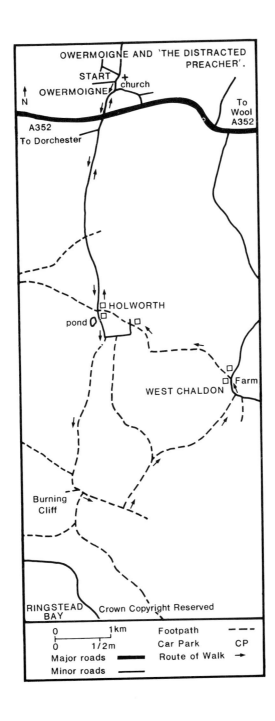

OWERMOIGNE AND 'THE DISTRACTED PREACHER'.

START
OWERMOIGNE
church

N

To Wool A352

A352
To Dorchester

HOLWORTH

pond

West Chaldon

Farm

Burning Cliff

RINGSTEAD BAY   Crown Copyright Reserved

0	1km	Footpath — — —
0	1/2m	Car Park CP
Major roads ▬▬▬		Route of Walk →
Minor roads ——		

9

Sutton Poyntz, White Horse Down and 'The Trumpet Major'

Walk distance: 4 miles

Hardy was fascinated by everything to do with the Napoleonic wars. As he grew up at Bockhampton, only a few miles from the threatened Wessex coast, the events of the long wars were still fresh in the minds of many around him. In the Preface to his novel, *The Trumpet Major*, Hardy says how much the story owes to this early eager listening: 'The external incidents which direct its course are mostly an unexaggerated reproduction of the recollections of old persons well known to the author in childhood.' Within his own family the wars were a frequent topic of conversation as his grandfather had been a volunteer. The volunteers, like the Home Guard in 1940, were to be England's last defence if, as was hourly expected, Napoleon launched his invading army from Boulogne. The most anxious years were those Hardy describes in the novel, immediately prior to 1805, before the threat of invasion was lifted by the victory at Trafalgar.

High on the downs above the Wessex coast the beacon keepers lived in make-shift huts, ready to light their signal fires if the French fleet were sighted. One night, tension mounted to such a pitch that the beacons were mistakenly lit. Women and children were packed into wagons and sent inland. The volunteers, Hardy's grandfather among them, marched to defend Weymouth. But for a moment his grandfather had hesitated, fearing for his wife and children. He finally decided he must go and fight only to hear, with immense relief, that the French had not landed after all. Hardy tells his story in a poem *The Alarm*.

When Hardy was eight, he was rummaging in a cupboard when he came across some copies of a periodical his grandfather had subscribed to during the wars. In the *Life* of Hardy written by his second wife (with, of course, Hardy's assistance) we read how greatly he was impressed by their 'melodramatic prints of serried ranks, crossed bayonets, huge knapsacks and dead bodies'. Another reminder met his gaze each time he looked out of his bedroom window: the memorial to Admiral Hardy, Captain of *Victory* and probably a distant relation, rising above Black Down.

No doubt his imagination was fired by tales of the glitter and excitement when the allied troops mustered on the downs to be reviewed by the King before embarkation. He heard too how the visits of George III and his family to Weymouth turned the sleepy little town into a hive of bustle and gaiety. The quiet chalk downs overlooking Weymouth and Portland Roads saw it all. The people in the remote villages tucked in their hollows suddenly found themselves caught up in the world's great affairs. It is the story of these simple people, who share in the making of history although their names go unrecorded, that Hardy tells in *The Trumpet Major*.

The story centres around one small village, 'Overcombe.' Although no downland village in the area has all the features Hardy attributes to Overcombe, its characteristics are, as usual, 'drawn from the real'. Hardy has in mind the church at Bincombe, the mill at Upwey and the manor house at Poxwell. But the village which must have influenced him most is Sutton Poyntz whose atmosphere and setting is exactly that of the novel. (There is a real Overcombe but it is not near the downs.)

Again Hardy was concerned that the events taking place near Overcombe should be described as accurately as possible. While at Sturminster Newton he had begun reading for the background of the novel. In 1877 he wrote to Mrs

Chatteris, daughter of Admiral Hardy, to verify some facts in her father's life. After the move to Upper Tooting, he continued his researches in the British Museum. To refresh his recollections of the countryside he visited Weymouth again.

Our walk along these beautiful and historic downs was very familiar to Hardy. In the steps of the characters in *The Trumpet Major* we cross the famous White Horse Down where a huge figure of George III on horseback is carved out of the turf. And we explore Sutton Poyntz, home of the novel's demure heroine, Anne Garland, and her two lovers, the ever-faithful John Loveday and his dashing sailor brother, Bob. The walk is about four miles round and we start and finish by the mill pond at Sutton Poyntz. Sutton Poyntz is a small village within an arm of the downs, seven miles south of Dorchester. From Dorchester, take the A354 Weymouth road. Turn left for Preston at Broadwey. Opposite the Ship Inn in Preston take the left turn for Sutton Poyntz. Dick Dewy and Fancy Day stopped at the Ship for tea in *Under the Greenwood Tree*. Another interesting approach is to follow the A352 from Wareham, through Wool. Over the old bridge in Wool you will see the manor house, now a hotel, where Tess spent her honeymoon with Angel Clare. At Warmwell crossroads take the A353 in the direction of Weymouth which runs along the seaward side of the downs.

This road takes you through Poxwell where you can see the Tudor manor upon which Hardy models 'Oxwell Hall', the home of Squire Derriman in *The Trumpet Major*. The wall round the outer courtyard has a porter's house over the gateway just as Hardy describes it. In Preston, turn right opposite the Ship for Sutton Poyntz. Before the village, the road forks. Go right for Springhead and park in the village. The bus from Weymouth stops here.

Sutton Poyntz is an enchanting village. The placid water of the mill pond is shaded by drooping willows and only slightly ruffled by flotillas of hungry ducks. Small stone bridges cross the stream to a row of tiled and thatched cottages framed by the green curve of the downs.

The figure of George III carved on the downs above Weymouth, covering more than an acre. In The Trumpet Major *John Loveday takes Anne to see 'forty navvies at work' removing the turf to make the figure.*

Our walk starts from the mill pond. Pass the Springhead Inn on your right and turn left over a bridge. Turn immediately left again to walk between the pond and the cottages towards the mill. In *The Trumpet Major* Anne Garland lives with her widowed mother in part of the mill house. Hardy describes the scene from Anne's window, still very much as we can see it today as we walk by the pond: 'Immediately before her was the large, smooth mill-pond, overfull, and intruding into the hedge and into the road. . . . Behind this a steep slope rose high into the sky, merging in a wide and open down, now littered with sheep newly shorn. . . .'.

You come to another bridge on the left. Keep straight on, past the bridge, along a footpath which takes you into a quiet green world between the back of the massive mill and some picturesque cottages. By a house called Blue Shutters you will see an old iron water pump. Turn left opposite the pump and cross a bridge to walk up the narrow lane between the mill and the mill house. At some time a thrifty miller has set old millstones as a path to connect the two buildings. Miller Loveday, whose house Anne and her mother share, has the same idea. 'In the court in front were two worn-out mill-stones, made useful again by being let in level with the ground. Here people stood to smoke and consider things in muddy weather; and cats slept on the clean surfaces when it was hot.' Turn left, round the mill and you will see a hoist like the one Bob uses in our story to escape from the press gang, and the doors in the wall 'one above the other, the upper enabling a person to step out upon nothing at a height of ten feet from the ground.'

One morning Anne looks from her window to see that the downs above the village are dotted with tents and that 'A number of soldiers were busily engaged in making a zig-zag path down the incline from the camp to the river head at the back of the house...'. That is our way. Keep straight on through the village with the mill pond again on your left. Turn right following the public footpath sign. A few yards down the lane on the left you come to the entrance to Hunt's Timber Yard. Turn left following the public footpath sign and cross the yard of Hunt's Timber Buildings and go over the stile ahead into the field. The path leads straight ahead over the field then bears a little right to a stile. Climb the stile and you leave the lush green of the valley behind you. Rough downland grasses wave in the wind which blows sharper and fresher now. Follow the path as it bears a little right, then uphill through patches of gorse and heather. As we climbed the hill one warm September afternoon, summer lingered on these southern slopes; a few late harebells nodded among the finer grass and small brown butterflies fluttered above the flat blue heads of the meadow scabious.

The mill-pond at Sutton Poyntz. As Hardy describes it in The
Trumpet Major, *the water is 'stealing away, like Time, under the
dark arch . . .'*

Go through a gate and follow the terraced path through
another gate to the highest point of the downs. At the top you
will see a tumulus, or burial mound, to the left of the path.
This is probably where Hardy imagined Anne Garland standing to watch the review of the allied troops. Today the armies
have gone, but the countryside is unchanged. Hardy describes
her view: 'It was a clear day with little wind stirring, and the
view from the downs, one of the most extensive in the
county, was unclouded. The eye swept over the wave washed
town, and the bay beyond, and the Isle, with its pebble bank,
lying on the sea to the left of these, like a great crouching
animal tethered to the mainland. On the extreme east of the
marine horizon, St Aldhelm's Head closed the scene, the sea
to the southward of that point glaring like a mirror under the
sun'. Looking inland we can see the beacon hills: Rainbarrow

on 'Egdon', Bulbarrow, Nettlecombe Tout, Dogbury Hill, and, far away, Black Down where the Hardy monument now stands. The long line of the Ridgeway runs white across the downs just as it did when Anne watched the troops moving along it. Close by are the ruins of a large building. Perhaps Hardy saw these as the remains of the barn which John Loveday tells Anne is being used as a temporary hospital. Huge military reviews, often two or three miles of troops stretching east and west along the Ridgeway, took place several times on the downs during the wars with Napoleon. Hardy merges them all into one for the purposes of the novel.

From the tumulus, go through the first gate on the right (ignore the next gate on our left) and follow the path as it bears right along the crest of the downs. (This path is now part of the Dorset Coast Path and is signposted 'Inland Route to Osmington'.) You come to another gate and our way is straight on. But first a look at George III. Go through the gate but turn immediately right following the sign to the White Horse. A little path leads over the top of a tumulus and continues beside a row of windswept thorn bushes. At the end of the field go over the fence and follow the track left for a few yards just over the brow of the hill and there you are standing on George III's hat! This enormous figure covers more than an acre. In our novel, John Loveday takes Anne to see 'forty navvies at work' removing the turf to make the figure. Anne wanders happily all over it but the bashful John 'remained all the time in a melancholy attitude within the rowel of his Majesty's right spur'. The Isle of Portland lies almost directly ahead. From Portland Bill Anne watches *Victory*, with Bob on board, sail past.

Retrace your steps beside the hedge, over the tumulus to the gate. Following the sign for Osmington and Poxwell walk along the top of the field. Go through the gate and turn right down the good path signposted Osmington. From the downs Osmington village appears as a small cluster of houses round a church tower half-buried in a wooded cleft in the hillside. As you follow the path downhill you lose sight of the village altogether. The hillsides beyond Osmington are carefully terraced with long strips of land running between the embankments. Saxon tribes evidently settled here as these strips or 'lynchets' were part of their farming methods. Each householder was allotted his share of strips, sometimes well scattered, the dwellings being grouped together in the village. The priest's share was known as his glebe land. Over on the right, beyond Sutton Poyntz, is a reminder of an earlier people, the concentric rings of Chalbury hill fort built during the Iron Age. The many barrows and tumuli scattered about on the downs were built over their dead.

Our way burrows between hedges thick with brambles and bright with red hawthorn berries. Closer to the village you are sheltered by willows and elderberries. Follow the lane through a gate into Osmington village. Just past the first turning on the left look for a water pump to the right of the road complete with handle and stone trough. (This may be buried in the brambles in Summer.) The lane on the right, past the pump, signposted Sutton Poyntz, is our return route but Osmington is too good to rush past.

This lovely village with its honey-coloured stone walls and deep-eaved cottages delighted John Constable. The artist brought his wife to spend their honeymoon at the vicarage and painted several pictures of the village. You come to the

Looking over Weymouth Bay to Portland 'lying on the sea . . . like a great crouching animal tethered to the mainland.'

church of St Osmund (nephew of William the Conqueror, after whom the village is named) on the right. The church is full of interest and Hardy no doubt appreciated the homely verse that is inscribed on a monument on the north wall of the chancel which reads:

> MANS: LIFE:
> MAN: IS: A GLAS: LIFE IS:
> AS: WATER: THATS: WEAKLY:
> WALLD: ABOUT: SINNE: BRIN
> GS: IN: DEATH: DEATH: BREA:
> KES: THE GLAS: SO: RUNS:
> THE: WATER: OUT:

The local Lords of the Manor in the sixteenth century were the Warham family and as you leave the church you will see the picturesque ruins of their Tudor manor house beside the churchyard. Hardy may have had the site of this manor in mind as the situation for Oxwell Hall in *The Trumpet Major*. Anne, sent by her mother on regular visits to Squire Derriman to collect a newspaper would have found this a reasonable distance to walk from Sutton Poyntz. When escaping from the unwelcome attentions of his son, Festus, she is forced to take a longer way home over the downs round the back of the military encampment.

Take the very narrow footpath between low stone walls opposite the church. Turn left when you come to the lane, then left again. Now we have rejoined the first lane we followed through Osmington by a pretty cottage which is an antique shop and Post Office combined. Turn right and retrace our earlier route to the lane, now on the left, which is signposted Sutton Poyntz and waymarked with a yellow arrow. Use the yellow arrows on gateposts as guides on this return route to Sutton Poyntz. The lane leads you to a gate. Through the gate you enter a field and have a splendid view of George III over on the down on your right. He is riding, rather unfortunately in the townsmen's opinion, *away* from Weymouth! Cross the field to another gate. (Check the yellow waymarks.) Be careful at this point. Cross the field ahead to the hedge and then turn right with the hedge on your left. Look for a small stile in the bottom corner of the field on your left. Climb the wooden stile and step over a stone stile just after it to walk across the next field with the little Jordan stream on your right. Keep straight on through the next gate and over the meadow with the stream still on your right and Sutton Poyntz directly ahead. When you have gone through another gate, the path bears right to cross the stream, then a little left to lead up to a gate. Keep straight on to a stile. Over the stile the path leads past a farmyard to bring you quickly back to the Springhead road. Turn right for the mill pond in Sutton Poyntz.

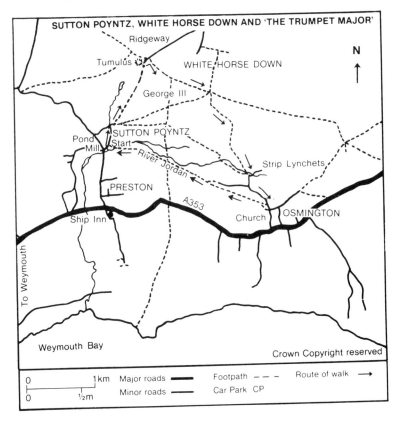

THE WALK IN BRIEF *(see previous page)*
Distance: four miles.

From the mill pond, Sutton Poyntz, turn left over second bridge. Keep straight on round the back of the mill. Turn left opposite the house Blue Shutters, then left past the mill. Walk straight on past the mill pond. Turn right at Public Footpath sign. After a few yards turn left through timber yard. Cross stile, over field, over another stile onto the downs. Keep uphill, through two gates to top of the downs. Just past a burial mound on left go through first gate on right. At next gate turn immediately right down side of field. Go over the fence, then a few yards left to see figure of George III. Return to gate, turn right and at next gate, bear right downhill to Osmington. Walk through village to church. Take footpath opposite church, then turn left and left again to rejoin earlier road. Turn right and retrace steps to lane on left signposted Sutton Poyntz with yellow waymarking. Follow this through several fields (look for yellow waymarks) – be careful at second field as the waymarked stile is over the field to your right – to cross the Jordan stream, past a farmyard to Springhead road. Turn right for mill pond in Sutton Poyntz.

10

Wimborne Minster, Milborne St Andrew and 'Two on a Tower'

Walk distance: 3 miles

At the end of October 1880, Hardy fell seriously ill. His doctor considered that if he was to lie still for six months he might be able to avoid an operation. So he dictated to Emma the story he had just begun for *Harper's Magazine*, *The Laodicean*. Emma worked bravely and by May 1881 a draft of the novel was finished. The same month Hardy felt well enough to walk on Wandsworth Common. The lease on their house had expired and prompted by the severity of his illness and the feeling that city life 'forced ordinary productions from his pen' Hardy began to look for a house in the country. Again his thoughts turned homewards to his beloved Dorset.

They lost no time and on the 25 June they moved to the outskirts of the little country town of Wimborne Minster. They leased 'Llanherne', in The Avenue, (now Avenue Road.) Although this was in the low-lying east side of the town not far from the Stour, it was close to the station. Since 1860 Wimborne had become the most important railway junction in Dorset and the Hardys could now be in London in four hours which was an important consideration for them. Their house still stands, a substantial brick villa framed today in flowering cherry trees. In a poem written in 1918, Hardy recalls that they looked out of their front windows on two rows of newly-planted limes 'thin in bough'. With a true countryman's delight Hardy records 'Our garden has all sorts of old-fashioned flowers in full bloom: Canterbury Bells, blue and white, and Sweet Williams of every variety, strawberries and cherries that are ripe, currants and gooseberries that are almost ripe, peaches that are green, and apples that are decidedly immature.' The garden was large and included a carriage house and stables. The stable wall was wreathed with a vine forming a sheltered place for Hardy to sit and write on sunny days. He remarks that the vine 'hangs in long arms over my head nearly to the ground. The sun tries to shine through the green leaves, making a green light on the paper, the tendrils twisting in every direction in gymnastic endeavours to find something to lay hold of.'

As early as 1875, Hardy had considered Wimborne as a possible home. He must have found this pleasant town with its interesting old streets set in green meadows threaded by the Allen and the Stour attractive. And Wimborne's glory, its homely many-coloured Minster cast a spell over him. While house-hunting, 'he entered the Minster at ten at night, having seen a light within, and sat in a stall listening to the organist practising, while the rays from the musician's solitary candle streamed across the arcades.'

Wimborne Minster, with its Saxon foundations supporting heavy Norman arches is so old, and so rich in history that it can afford not to take itself too seriously! Hardy was as delighted as we are today to see the little figure of a Quarter Jack, dressed as a grenadier, standing high up outside a window on the north wall of the west tower of the Minster regularly marking each quarter hour. He begins a poem *Copying Architecture in an old Minster* with a verse that captures the sound of the jack:

> 'How smartly the quarters of the hour march by
> That the jack-o'clock never forgets;
> Ding-dong; and before I have traced a cusp's eye,
> Or got the true twist of the ogee over,
> A double ding-dong ricochetts'.

Hardy, as an architect, was interested too in the extensive restoration work being undertaken at the Minster. This included tidying its immediate surroundings by uprooting old

The Quarter Jack on the north wall of the West of Tower of Wimborne Minster – Hardy's 'jack o'clock'.

gravestones and using some for paving and laying others flat. Inspired by this and influenced, I think, by the Minster's own refusal to be over-serious, Hardy wrote one of his few humorous poems, *The Levelled Churchyard.* A displaced ghost complains:

'Here's not a modest maiden elf
But dreads the final Trumpet
Lest half of her should rise herself,
And half some sturdy strumpet!'

Inside the Minster, a detail that caught Hardy's eye in St George's chapel was the arms of the Fitz Piers family, once the lords of the manor of Hinton Martell. Hardy was to give this name to the fickle doctor in *The Woodlanders*.

Apart from the pleasure he derived from the town and its Minster, Hardy enjoyed discovering more of the Dorset countryside. A month after their arrival in Wimborne, Hardy and Emma drove out to visit Badbury Rings, a large Iron Age earthwork a few miles to the north-west. On the way they passed the conspicuous tower in the grounds of a private estate five miles west of Wimborne, Charborough Park. Hardy was already contemplating a story featuring an astronomer – on the night of their arrival at Llanherne he notes that they watched Tebbutt's comet from the garden – and he must have considered the possibility of using a tower similar to that at Charborough as a suitable observatory for his stargazer. So when he received a request in October 1881 from the editor of the *Atlantic Monthly* for a serial for the following year, Hardy promptly sent him the outline of a novel given the working title of *Two on a Tower*. Although not one of Hardy's best known stories, this is a touching and powerful novel prefiguring in its love passages the great tragedies he was to write later.

Just as in the *The Return of the Native* Hardy had set human passions against the brooding presence of Egdon Heath, now he proposed setting human love, warm and passionate, against the immensity of the cosmic universe. The tower not only serves a practical purpose as an observatory, it is the means of isolating two human figures from the rest of humanity, framing them literally against the sky. Lady Viviette Constantine of Welland, on whose estate the tower is presumed to be, falls passionately in love with the handsome young astronomer, Swithin St Cleeve who she discovers observing the stars from the top of a tower on her estate. He is ten years younger than Viviette but she is beautiful and wealthy and he returns her love. Viviette's love can survive all difficulties and contrivances, but Swithin's cannot. What Hardy terms 'time's napping chisel' ages Viviette and finally brings about her tragedy. Throughout much of his work Hardy stresses the effects of time, slipping away unobserved but with profound effects on human life.

Hardy sets *Two on a Tower* in his immediate surroundings, once again drawing his inspiration 'from the real'. Wimborne appears as a 'Warborne' in the novel. Swithin St Cleeve is educated at the grammar school and Wimborne station with its convenient access to London and the West Country is used frequently by characters in the story. However, he treats the setting of Welland and Welland House where most of the action takes place with some imaginative freedom. On his own map of Wessex he marks the village near Charborough Park. This is conveniently close to Wimborne for his characters and satisfies some of the needs of the plot. Hardy required an estate with a manor house very close to a church, and of course, a tower. He had not visited Charborough (he records his first visit when he was over eighty) but from Hutchins *History of Dorset* he could gather some of the information he needed: that some old village houses around the church had been destroyed leaving the church isolated and that Charborough Tower, with its Tuscan features, could be climbed for the 'pleasurable effect . . . to be derived from looking into four counties' or, in Swithin's case to use as an observatory. But the novel convinces because Hardy is so exact in his descriptions of nature, of the rise and fall of the land and all its historical features, of the paths his characters tread and the trees that shade their homes. These features he had to observe for himself. So he establishes his tower, 'Rings-Hill Speer' on an old Iron Age fort, Weatherby Castle, which is crowned by an obelisk already and uses the surrounding countryside and Milborne St Andrew close by as the setting of the story. There is a possibility also that Hardy was deliberately masking his use of Charborough Park.

Today, a pleasant walk of about three miles will reward you with fascinating insights into the novel. Our starting point is the attractive village of Milborne St Andrew, about three miles to the north of the road running between Bere Regis and Puddletown. Turn off the A35 to follow the A354 in the direction of Salisbury for six miles. The road runs through the centre of the village once famous for its coaching inns. Pass one of these, the Royal Oak on your left and turn almost immediately right down Chapel Street where there is room to park near the school. Walk on down Chapel Street and turn right to walk up the lane to St Andrews Church. This lovely little church dates from 1150 and I feel that Hardy could well have had St Andrews in mind when he describes Welland church. Like Welland, St Andrews is 'semi-Norman' in style. The reset chancel arch is a beautiful example of a transitional Norman arch, just beginning to rise to a point. And like Welland too, the arch is decorated with zig-zag 'multitudinous notchings'. The south doorway dates from the same period and is decorated with a double row of chevrons and although Hardy never mentions it, the church has a lovely simple Norman font, ornamented with a cable design.

From the church return down the lane to meet Chapel Street. Walk straight on and turn right to cross a stream and follow the road as it bears a little left and uphill to pass a long, low thatched cottage. Although not where Hardy describes it – we shall see 'Welland Bottom' later – this house reminded me of Mrs Martin's home in our novel: 'a venerable thatched house, whose enormous roof, broken up by dormers as big as haycocks, could be seen even in the twilight.'

At the top of the hill (this part of the village is called Little England) a lane joins the road from the right. Turn right and follow this for a few yards. When you come to a grassy triangle, turn left to follow a lane marked 'Unsuitable for Motors'. The lane leads you past a farm then through quiet green countryside, along the side of a shallow valley. The lane turns right but our way is through the gate straight ahead, indicated with yellow waymarking. Now you will see Weatherby Castle, or Iron Age fort-'Rings-Hill' in the novel – across the fields, surrounded by farmland, just as Hardy describes it: 'a circular isolated hill ... with remains of an outer and an inner vallum, a winding path leading up between their overlapping ends by an easy ascent'. Go through the gate and follow the field path straight ahead, then turn left to climb to the top. I climbed the embankments of the fort in late April and the ridges glowed with cowslips. I felt sure Hardy would have enjoyed them too as he was particularly fond of them. He notes in the *Life* that they seem to emit light, like glow-worms.

Unlike the Rings-Hill in the novel, the top is not shrouded with fir trees but young oaks and beeches. But, like Viviette and Swithin, you still have to pick your way through brambles to find the obelisk in the centre. This is a tapering brick column surmounted by a ball. Now crumbling and forgotten, it was erected in 1761 to honour Edmund Morton Pleydell, Lord of the Manor of Milborne St Andrew. Impossible to climb at any time, and quite useless as an observatory, we must imagine in its place the windowed tower with the staircase that Hardy describes in the novel modelled on the tower at Charborough.

We retrace our steps down the hill and along the field path to the gate opening into the lane but first pause for a moment to look down at the valley threaded by a stream beneath. It appears, as Hardy pictures it in evening light: 'gently concave; with the exception of tower and hill there were no points on which late rays might linger; and hence the dish-shaped fifty acres of tilled land assumed a uniform hue of shade quite suddenly'. If you look over to the right you will see the 'little dell which occurred quite unexpectedly on the other side of the field fence' which I feel sure Hardy imagined as Welland Bottom close to Little Welland. Here Swithin's grandmother had her home. Her house would form a natural meeting place for workers living in outlying cottages to meet for choir practice as the church is almost a mile away. Hardy draws his rural characters with his usual insight, presenting them as individuals and although amusing, they are never caricatures. Among them is Hezzy Biles who describes Swithin in one pithy sentence as 'planned, cut out, and finished for the delight of 'ooman!'

Return to the gate and turn left to follow the lane through a gate and across a stream. The bridleway goes straight on here, but we turn immediately right over a stile to follow the stream back in the direction of Milborne St Andrew. With the stream on your right, follow the path which runs close to it, beside a fringe of bushes. This reminded me of the walk Viviette takes to Little Welland to exercise her house-dog, a large St Bernard. 'The distance was but short, and she returned along a narrow lane, divided from the river by a hedge, through whose leafless twigs the ripples flashed silver lights into her eyes.' Ahead you will see the tower of St Andrews Church. After going through a gate our path runs a little right to meet a path past Manor Farm. This still impressive building is all that is left of the Manor after a disastrous fire early in the nineteenth century. You walk between two old stone gateposts and across a meadow to the foot of the lane leading to the church. Keep straight on back to Chapel Street.

THE WALK IN BRIEF
Distance: three miles.

Park in Chapel Street in Milborne St Andrew. With your back to the main road walk down Chapel Street and turn right to visit church. Walk back to junction with Chapel Street and keep straight on for a short distance. Turn right then follow road as it bears left uphill. At top turn right down lane for a few yards then turn left to follow lane marked 'Unsuitable for Motors'. Before lane turns right keep straight ahead through gate marked by footpath sign and yellow waymarks. Follow field path straight ahead then turn left to climb Weatherby hill fort. Retrace steps to lane, turn left, cross stream and bear right over stile. Turn right to walk with stream on right towards Milborne St Andrew. Go through gate and follow path a little right past Manor Farm. Walk between stone gateposts and over field to Chapel Street. Distance: three miles.

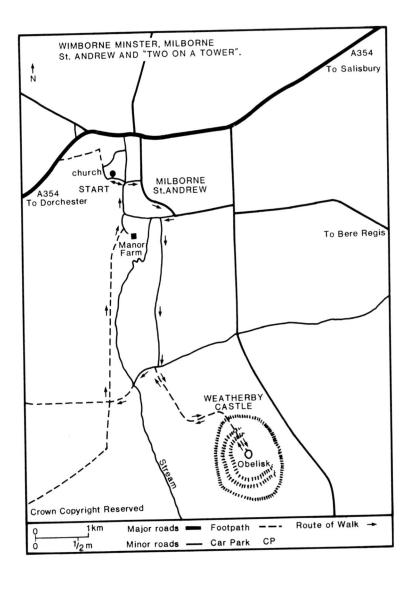

WIMBORNE MINSTER, MILBORNE
St. ANDREW AND "TWO ON A TOWER".

N

A354
To Salisbury

church

START

MILBORNE
St. ANDREW

A354
To Dorchester

To Bere Regis

Manor
Farm

WEATHERBY
CASTLE

Obelisk

Stream

Crown Copyright Reserved

| 0 | 1km | Major roads ▬▬ | Footpath ‑ ‑ ‑ | Route of Walk → |
| 0 | ½ m | Minor roads ▬ | Car Park | CP |

11

Dorchester and 'The Mayor of Casterbridge'

Walk distance: about 4 miles

In June, 1883, Hardy and Emma moved again, renting 7 Shire Hall Place, in the centre of Dorchester. Perhaps half unconsciously, Hardy, now forty three, was coming home. His parents, to whom he was devoted, still lived at Bockhampton close by. He may have been influenced also by his growing friendship with the poet William Barnes who was now rector of Winterborne Came, a small village just south of Dorchester. In the midst of the rich and varied life of the county town he knew so well, Hardy wrote one of his greatest novels, *The Mayor of Casterbridge*.

'Casterbridge' was Hardy's name for Dorchester. The novel is strong and vivid because he weaves into its fabric so much of his own deep knowledge of the town. Surrounding earthworks tell of human habitation two thousand years before the Romans came to set out the streets and confine them within high raised walls. They established too the military traditions of the town, still important today.

Throughout its history, the small assize town has witnessed countless human dramas, some famous like the visit of Judge Jeffreys after the Monmouth Rebellion, and the conviction of the Tolpuddle Martyrs; others day-to-day events that have left no mark on history but which, to Hardy, were just as important. There were plenty of these for Dorchester was the meeting place, market and economic centre for all the surrounding countryside. From his house, only a few steps away from where the markets were held around Cornhill, Hardy missed nothing. With a touch of quizzical humour he acknowledged this after he had been presented, many years later, with the freedom of Dorchester. 'I may be allowed to confess that the freedom of the Borough of Dorchester did seem to me at first something that I had possessed a long while . . . for when I consider the liberties I have taken with its ancient walls, streets and precincts through the medium of the printing press, I feel I have treated its external features with the hand of freedom indeed.' But Hardy goes further. He does not only concern himself with the appearance of the town. In his study of the Mayor of Casterbridge, corn merchant Henchard, locked in bitter rivalry with the brilliant Farfrae, Hardy reveals the whole economic basis of the town's society before the repeal of the Corn Laws. Buying and selling was a gamble, depending ultimately upon the weather at harvest time. A bad guess could bring ruin to a merchant, a bad harvest starvation to the poor.

Dorchester is still fairly well confined within the limits of the embankment of its Roman walls to the north, west and south, and a branch of the Frome river to the east. From a distance the town appears as Hardy described it 'compact as a box of dominoes'. There are many fascinating places to see and this walk round the town needs a full day. We begin and end at the Top o' Town car park. This is just beyond the western end of High West Street. If you are entering Dorchester from the east from the A35, drive straight through the town, across the junction with the Yeovil and Weymouth roads, and the car park entrance is a few yards further on the right. From the car park, turn left and walk towards the junction and the top of Dorchester's main thoroughfare, High West Street. (Further down this becomes High East Street.) On the left is a memorial statue of Hardy. The sculptor was Eric Kennington. The grass and plants round the feet of the statue represent Egdon Heath. Behind Hardy's seated figure, leading north, is one of Dorchester's well-known avenues or 'walks'. They are still as he described them: 'The stockade of gnarled trees which framed in Casterbridge was itself an avenue, standing on a low green bank or escarpment, with a ditch yet visible without … the ancient defences of the town, planted as a promenade'.

The view down High West Street is an interesting blend of Georgian bows and elegant doorways, older cottages and modern façades, the grey stone of the churches and walls softened with ferns and lichens. Early in the nineteenth century there were more old houses like the ones Hardy describes: 'Timber houses with overhanging storeys, whose small-paned lattices were screened by dimity curtains on a draw string, and under whose barge boards old cobwebs waved in the breeze'. But Hardy's Tea Room which you pass at the top of the street, with its black and white half-timbered walls filled with brick nogging, still fits that description.

Walk down High West Street and take the first narrow turning on your left, Glyde Path Road. As you turn the corner, the large building on the right is the Shire Hall where the Tolpuddle Martyrs were tried. High up on the wall you will see the original name of the lane you have just entered, as you might expect, 'Shire Hall Lane'. Above, on a water pipe is the date of the building, 1797. Hardy lived at 7 Shire Hall Place. The house has been demolished, but if you turn left just past the County Laboratory and go up the steps to the corner of the car park, you will be standing on the approximate site. A few yards further down Shire Hall Lane you come to Colliton House. Hardy models Lucetta's home, High Place Hall, in the novel, upon this large grey stone house. If you turn left for a few yards to look at the front of the house you will see that it is still very much as Hardy describes it: 'The house was entirely of stone, and formed an example of dignity without great size', it possessed 'the characteristics of a country mansion – birds nests in its chimneys, damp nooks where fungi grew, and irregularities of surface direct from Nature's trowel'.

Follow Glyde Path Road downhill past some old houses until it turns left. Now leave the lane, and walk straight on down some steep steps, shaded by chestnut and sycamore trees, to a minor road opposite a long low stone and brick thatched cottage. In former days when trade was brisk, this was the hangman's cottage. Hardy features the house, still called 'Hangman's Cottage' in his short story *The Withered Arm.*

Bear right to cross a bridge over the Frome and walk along the river bank. Here, as you walk along a precise line between town and country – the green meadows dotted with cattle on your left and the river protecting the town on your right – little has changed since Hardy wrote: 'Casterbridge . . . was a place deposited in the block upon a cornfield. There was no suburb in the modern sense . . . reapers at work among the sheaves nodded to acquaintances standing on the pavement corner.' As the cliff behind the Frome steepens look through the trees for the stone archway of the prison above. Here public hangings took place. Hardy writes: 'at executions the waiting crowd stood in a meadow immediately before the drop out of which the cows had been temporarily driven to give the spectators room'. At the age of sixteen, Hardy watched a woman hanged there, a sight which affected him deeply.

Follow the river to Town Bridge at the foot of High East Street. At the time of the novel this was a brick bridge and the meeting place for outcasts and failures of the worst character. Look left down the road and you will see Grey's Bridge. Here down and outs also gathered but, Hardy explains, they were of the 'shabby-genteel' order. They tended to gaze sadly over the parapet into the water, whereas those on Town Bridge looked brazenly at passers by and complained they were 'down on their luck'. We now go through what was once the home of the destitute and the criminals of Casterbridge – along Mill Street or Mixen Lane as the area is called in the novel. Cross Town Bridge, and with the Old Malt House on your right, follow the footpath by the stream. The old Mill Street has been cleared and new houses built but at the time of the story it was a huddle 'of thatched and mud-walled houses by the sallows . . . the hiding place of those who were in distress and in debt and trouble of every kind'. The idea of the skimmity ride – effigies of victims were paraded for public mockery – was mooted in the local inn, Peters Finger.

The footpath leads you into Mill Street. Keep straight on and at the end of the street you come to the old mill and a bridge. Turn right, over the bridge (forbidden, a notice says, to 'locomotive traction engines and other ponderous carriages') and right again to walk past the mill along Holloway Road. There has been a mill here for over a thousand years as it is recorded in the Domesday Book in 1086. Through the efforts of the Mill Street Housing Society, formed in 1931, the Old Roller Flour Mills were purchased, converted into nine flats and a shop in 1940 and opened completely modernised as Mill Stream House in 1964. The building was remodelled with additions in 1986. There is a rather strange effigy in a wall to the right of the entrance dated 1590. Take the first turning left up Pound Lane to Fordington High Street. This is the 'Durnover' of the novel. Hardy called this district so from the Roman name for Dorchester, 'Durnovaria'. The old church of St George is on your left. Hardy often visited the church as a close friend of the Moule brothers whose father was rector here, and in later years came to services from his home at Max Gate. At the time of the novel, Durnover was still a farming district. 'Here wheat ricks overhung the old Roman street, and thrust their eaves against the church tower...'. The farms may not be so close today but we noticed a yard full of pigs grunting happily beneath the church wall.

From the church, walk round the top of the green opposite into South Walks Road. Turn right almost immediately down the gravel track in front of 27 South Walks Road. This leads to the open expanse of Salisbury Field, bordered on your left by a fine avenue of chestnuts. Cross to the chestnut avenue and bear right under their shade along the edge of the field. This is probably the route Fanny Robin took to the union workhouse in *Far from the Madding Crowd*. Keep straight ahead down Salisbury Street to High East Street, by Town Bridge.

Turn left along High East Street. Through narrow archways

The Kings Arms, Dorchester. In The Mayor of Casterbridge *Susan Henchard is able to see, through the curved bay window projecting over the pavement, the husband who had sold her many years before presiding as Mayor over 'a great public dinner of the gentle-people and such like leading folk'.*

are fascinating glimpses of cobbled yards and cottages, their gardens glowing with flowers. Hardy commented on 'this floral blaze' and added the gardens were 'backed by crusted grey stonework remaining from a yet remoter Casterbridge than the venerable one visible in the street'. The Royal British Legion Club you pass on your right is built on the site of the Tudor Three Mariners Inn of the novel. A little further on you reach the King's Arms which Hardy describes as 'the chief hotel in Casterbridge'. Inside the curved bay which projects over the pavement, Susan Henchard and her daughter Elizabeth Jane saw the husband who had sold her many years before, now Mayor of the town, at 'a great public dinner of the gentle-people and such like leading folk'. Hardy uses the King's Arms many times in novels and poems.

A narrow roadway divides the Corn Exchange, once the Market House and Town Hall, from the church of St Peter behind its curved wall, the Bow. At the time of the novel, 'the neighbouring Market House and Town Hall abutted against its next neighbour the church except in the lower storey, where an arched thoroughfare gave admittance to a large Square called Bull Stake'.

Opposite the Bow, at the top of South Street, stands the town pump erected in 1754 on the site of a more ancient Market House. All the gossips of the town gathered here. Hardy imagines Lucetta's home, High Place Hall, on the corner, overlooking this crossroads, the heart of Dorchester. From her window she has a splendid view of all the life of the town below, including the twice-weekly market. It was a busy, noisy scene with carriers' vans 'drawn up on each side of the street in close file . . . horses tied in rows, their forelegs on the pavement' and 'any inviting recess utilized by pig-dealers as a pen for their stock'. Among the animals moved farmers and merchants, expressing their feelings in their own individual fashion. There was little need for words, 'here the face, the arms, the hat, the stick, the body throughout spoke equally with the tongue'.

Every February Dorchester held its important Candlemas

Holy Trinity churchyard, Dorchester. In this pleasant green oasis, the ruined corn merchant Henchard is set up in a small seed shop.

Fair, when stalls stretched under the walls of St Peter's, round the town pump, up and down the High Street and into South Street and North Square. This was the chief hiring fair of the year when workers seeking fresh employment stood wearing dress appropriate to their occupation hoping to be engaged. In *Far from the Madding Crowd* Hardy describes Gabriel Oak's visit to the fair. Meeting with no success as a bailiff he buys a shepherd's smock. Lucetta and Farfrae take pity on a young man forced to choose between accepting a place where he would be close to his sweetheart and caring for his old father who is now old and feeble and unwanted.

Turn down the lane with St Peter's church on your left, into North Square. Hardy calls this 'Bull Stake' because bulls were once fastened to a stake here and baited to make them tender. Hardy recalls seeing a man in the stocks which also stood in this square.

Turn left up Colliton Street, then about half way up the street, turn left again down Grey School Passage almost opposite No. 22. The little lane leads you back to the High Street. You go past Holy Trinity Churchyard, a green oasis edged by old cottages. In this pleasant sunny corner, Henchard was set up in a seed shop with Elizabeth Jane. Turn left down the High Street. Walk past the statue of William Barnes, over the road, and down South Street. A tall house, set back a little on your left, faced with red and grey bricks and now a branch of Barclays Bank was the model for Henchard's house in the novel. Further down on the left you come to some quaint almshouses founded in 1615 by Sir Robert Napier, called 'Nappers Mite'. The clock on the bracket above the arch leading to the courtyard was the subject of Hardy's first printed work, a letter to the local newspaper. The letter purported to be from the clock itself complaining that after it had been taken down for repair it had not been replaced.

A few yards past Nappers Mite, opposite the entrance to Hardye's Arcade look for the two plaques on the right at first floor level. The first indicates the house where William Barnes kept school and the second on the adjoining building marks Hicks' office where the young Hardy trained as an architect. Here Hardy began his long friendship with the Dorset poet and scholar.

When you reach the corner of South Street – notice the Victorian pillar box – cross over and walk down Weymouth Avenue. (In the direction of South Station). In about a quarter of a mile the high, grass-covered circular embankment of Maumbury Ring appears on your left. Go through the gate on your left to look at this astonishing amphitheatre. Possibly the scene of fertility rites in Neolithic times, it was used by the Romans for gladiatorial contests. During the civil wars it was a gun emplacement and in the eighteenth century a place of execution. Hardy uses the 'dismal privacy' which the great arena affords for secret, almost sinister meetings in the novel. When he was very young, Hardy was brought here to see effigies of the Pope and Cardinal Wiseman burned during the No-Popery riots. Cross the arena and over the embankment you come onto the road through an iron gate. Turn right and walk back towards Dorchester down Maumbury Road.

Go straight over the crossroads in front of the Great Western Hotel, then, just after the Hotel, turn right down a footpath at the side of the Borough Gardens. Turn left along West Walk, a beautiful avenue of chestnuts and sycamores. Here Henchard found a home for his rediscovered wife and daughter. The house faced west so that the long rays of the setting sun streamed through the green shutters of their ground-floor rooms. It was close to the Roman wall too and after crossing the top of Princes Street, you'll see part of the wall on the right. With the gateway of the Victorian barracks ahead, leave West Walk at the top of High West Street, and turn left for the car park.

If you have time, walk past Hardy's statue, a short distance down Colliton Avenue and look west at the great earthwork that dominates Dorchester, Poundbury, on whose flat top Henchard planned his own expensive entertainment for the citizens of Dorchester.

No visit to Dorchester is complete without a look at the Dorset County Museum in the High Street. Among many treasures, there is the Dorset Worthies room with a reconstruction of Hardy's study at Max Gate – notice the calendar set as Hardy always kept it at the date he first met Emma – and a collection of rural implements that throw much light on the daily lives of the characters in his work. A military museum is housed in the gateway to the Victorian barracks.

THE WALK IN BRIEF
Distance: about four miles.

From Top o' Town car park walk down High West Street. Turn first left down Glyde Path Road (Old Shire Hall Lane). When road turns left, keep straight on down the steps to minor road in front of Hangman's Cottage. Turn right over bridge and walk right, along the river bank to Town Bridge. Cross the road and continue along footpath by the river, down Mill Street to the mill and the bridge. Turn right over the bridge, to walk up Holloway Road. Take first left (Pound Street) to Fordington High Street.

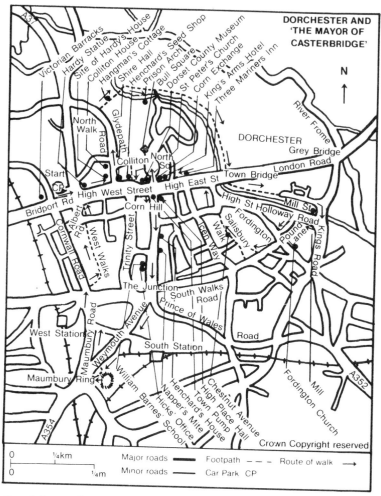

Bear left, round the green, into South Walks Road. Then immediately right down gravel track opposite 27 to Salisbury Field. Follow chestnut avenue to Salisbury Street, then to High East Street by Town Bridge. Turn left up High East Street, right just before St Peter's Church to North Square. Left up Colliton Street, then first left down footpath past Trinity Churchyard to High West Street. Cross the road and walk down South Street, over the jucntion and down Weymouth Avenue to Maumbury Ring. Take second road on your right (Maumbury Road) back towards Dorchester. Just past the Great Western Hotel turn right, then left along West Walk to the top of High West Street.

12

Melbury Osmond and the country of the first edition of 'The Woodlanders'

Life in the centre of Dorchester, interesting though it was, must have had its trying moments for Hardy, so much the quiet countryman. Finding no property in the area to suit himself and Emma as a permanent home he bought a plot of land about a mile south-east of the town in Fordington Field and designed his own house. He called it Max Gate after the keeper of a nearby turnpike cottage. Building operations, organised by his brother Henry, took eighteen months. Emma complained that the site was bleak and exposed so Hardy planted over two thousand small trees, mostly Austrian pines, to shield the house from the road. On 29 June, 1885, the Hardys slept at Max Gate for the first time. Now they had a home of their own which they were not to leave again except for their yearly visits to London.

In the peace of the countryside, surrounded by all the associations of his boyhood and early years, Hardy could retire to write the woodland story he had had in mind since the completion of *Far from the Madding Crowd* ten years previously. Again he turned to a part of the country which was very familiar to him for the background and setting of the novel, placing it in north Dorset around Melbury Osmond where his parents' families had once owned a fair amount of land. The theme of lost status due to loss of property runs through the novel. Another important theme was also a matter of deep concern to the Hardy family. Like so many country people they were life-holders; upon the expiry of a given number of lives their house at Bockhampton would 'fall in hand', that is become the property of the landowner, unless they were fortunate enough to be able to renew the lease. The failure of Giles Winterborne to do this in *The Woodlanders* is the root cause of his tragedy.

But there is a deeper note of sadness in the novel. Hardy is concerned with the pathos that can underlie the existence of even the most secluded folk. He describes 'Little Hintock', where most of the story takes place, as being 'one of those sequestered spots outside the gates of the world ... where, from time to time, dramas of a grandeur and unity truly Sophoclean are enacted in the real, by virtue of the concentrated passions and close-knit interdependence of the lives there'. In his tragedy, man was part of the whole of Nature's law which, with its stunted growth and blighted crops, proved on all sides what Hardy called 'The Unfulfilled Intention'. In the story, Grace Melbury watches her husband, Fitzpiers, ride off to visit another woman and wonders sadly 'if there were one world in the universe where the fruit had no worm, and marriage no sorrow'.

But *The Woodlanders* is a rich and rewarding novel. It contains some of Hardy's most beautiful descriptions of nature. There are forest scenes so evocative that you can smell the scent of woodsmoke and when Giles turns his cider press you can almost taste the sticky sweetness of the apples. The characters are subtly drawn and in the case of Marty South and Giles reach new heights of poetic expression. They are so close to the world of growing things that they speak at times 'the tongue of the trees and fruits and flowers themselves'.

Our walk takes us through the country where Hardy set the first edition of the novel. (In later editions he carefully changed the setting so that the main action of the story takes place three or four miles further east.) This is where the high chalklands of North Dorset overlook the Vale of Blackmore. Although not as densely wooded today, it is still a country of tree-covered slopes, oak, beech and ash predominating, and

Looking over the thatched roofs of Melbury Osmond to the church on the hill where Hardy's parents were married. The village is 'Great Hintock' in the first edition of The Woodlanders. *It is still a remote and peaceful hamlet, and cars must cross the watersplash in wet weather.*

gently curved valleys. Time moves slowly here. I felt I had stepped into Hardy's world – the world of the Great House with its omnipotent Lord or Lady, its wide parklands and villages clustering round its gates. I was not surprised to hear that many of the villagers still hold their houses on life-leases. From Melbury Osmond we cross the park, past the house where there is still a Lady of the Manor, to Evershot, Hardy's 'Evershead'. We return with a detour to Bubb Down, overlooking the Blackmore Vale, and Melbury Bubb, a tiny village tucked into the hillside below the Down, suggesting in its remoteness 'Little Hintock' with its 'gardens and orchards sunk in a concave, and, as it were, snipped out of the woodland'.

Melbury Osmond is a gem of a village. It lies in a quiet valley close to the A37, which runs north from Dorchester to Yeovil. Coming from the east, turn right at Dorchester's Top o' Town roundabout, at the top of High West Street, and follow the A37 along the Frome valley and over the Evershot crossroads. About three miles further you will see the left turn for Melbury Osmond. Follow the road through the village, turning left at a T-junction, then left again round to the south side of the church where there is room to park. When we first came here, the thick October morning mist was melting into dusky sunshine which highlighted the gold on the leaves of the chestnuts shading the churchyard and the honey colour of its old walls. The church of St Osmond stands high, its tower rising above a cluster of thatched roofs. Here Hardy's parents were married. The vicar told us the church had been altered but he pointed out to us two pictures of the interior as it was at the time of their wedding. Hardy's parents stood inside the chancel within a much larger arch and no doubt the quire played and sang in the little wooden gallery behind them.

Walk round the tower to the northern side of the church. Over the churchyard wall, is a thatched cottage. Here Hardy's mother, Jemima, lived before her marriage. Jemima's mother, Elizabeth Swetman, had married a poor man, George Hand. Her father considered she had married beneath her and left her nothing in his will. After her husband's early death, Elizabeth struggled against great poverty to bring up several children. But Jemima was quick and intelligent. She acquired a store of local knowledge and folklore and recognised the value of books and education. She prompted Hardy's early study of the classics as the necessary basis of a professional career and shared with him a sense of fun and a delight in the open air. Many of her beliefs and the stories she told as they walked on the heath found their place in his writing.

From the church, walk down the village and cross the bridge over the stream. Soon after the publication of the first edition of *The Woodlanders* the village was identified by

Hardy as 'Great Hintock' of the novel. Later he changed the location, but Melbury Osmond can still claim to be 'King's Hintock', mentioned several times in his work, and the background to his short story *Interlopers at the Knap*. Melbury Osmond is also the background of *Betty, Countess of Wessex* one of the stories Hardy included in his *Group of Noble Dames*.

Follow the lane ahead to a small group of cottages known as Town's End. The road turns right to Clammer's Gate, one of the entrances to the park. On the left, facing the gateway, is another house with associations with Hardy. A fine stone-built house, its mullioned windows surmounted by drip-stones, it was once the home of his grandparents. Hardy brought Emma here to sketch the house.

Today the house is called Monmouth Cottage. Hardy's short story *The Duke's Reappearance* explains the name. The story is based on a tradition that had been handed down in the Swetman family. It was said that late one night, shortly after the Duke's defeat at Sedgemoor, Christopher Swetman opened his door to give refuge to a tall, dark cavalry officer. The exhausted young man asked for a suit of yeoman's clothes in exchange for his own. Early next morning the stranger disappeared 'through Clammer's Gate by the road that crosses King's Hintock Park to Evershead'. He left behind foreign money, an Andrea Ferara sword which he had mentioned belonged to his grandfather, and portraits of King Charles and his Queen. Reports spread that the Duke, dressed as a countryman, had been captured but one night the stranger returned, collected the articles he had left, and disappeared again. Swetman always believed that his visitor was the Duke of Monmouth who had somehow escaped and that one of his officers had been executed in his place. A tall story? An old man who now lives in part of Monmouth Cottage says there is a dug-out, a mile or so down the lane which leads past the house towards the main road, where the Duke was successfully hidden.

In the steps of the mysterious visitor, go through Clammer's Gate into Melbury Park, or 'King's Hintock Park' to call it by Hardy's name. An avenue of evenly-spaced chestnut trees borders the way to the great house. Beyond the park on the left rise the wooded slopes of Bubb Down, and rolling away on the right are billowing masses of woodlands. In these woods Giles Winterborne makes his home in a deserted charcoal burner's cottage, 'one chimney hut', after his eviction from Little Hintock. Grace Melbury, escaping from her faithless husband, comes here to seek Giles' help. Grace arrives at the end of summer when 'after showers, creeping damps and twilight chills came up from the hollows'. She finds the hut, which Hardy describes so vividly 'a square cot of one storey only, sloping up on all sides to a chimney in the midst'. Inside, 'the room within was kitchen, parlour and

Monmouth Cottage at Town's End, Melbury Osmond. This was the home of the Swetmans, Hardy's maternal ancestors and the setting of his short story The Duke's Reappearance.

bedchamber all in one; the natural sandstone floor was worn into hills and dales by long treading, so that none of the furniture stood level, and the table slanted like a desk.'

Soon you will see Melbury House, or 'King's Hintock Court' ahead. It stands, grey and aloof, its neat rows of classically correct windows shaded by balustrades and shallow gables. Glimpses of tall twisting chimneys and narrow towers hint at an older wing of the house. In a hollow, to the left of the mansion, is the tiny church of Melbury Sampford. The contrast between the Great House and Giles' poor hut illustrated for us the tremendous gulf between rich and poor that characterised Hardy's Wessex. Probably Hardy did not have this house in mind as the home of Mrs. Charmond, the enigmatic lady of the manor in *The Woodlanders*. Her home 'built in a hole' is said to have been inspired by Turnworth House, now demolished. But the surrounding parkland and countryside is exactly right for our novel.

Perhaps Hardy heard from his mother the story of the ghosts of King's Hintock Court. In *The Woodlanders* the bark-rippers tell the story to Fitzpiers as they sit round their fire in the woods. It is 'the standard story of the spirits of the Two Brothers who had fought and fallen and had haunted King's Hintock Court till they were exorcised by the priest and compelled to retreat to a swamp, whence they were returning to their old quarters at the Court at the rate of a cock's stride every New Year's Day....'.

In front of the mansion you turn right, then keep to the lane marked public footpath as it bears left to lead you through the park gates close to Evershot. Walk down the lane ahead, past the lodge and follow the lane as it bears right in front of 'The Common' to lead you through Evershot. This is Hardy's 'Evershead'. In his novel *Tess of the d'Urbervilles*, Hardy brings Tess this way on her long walk from Flintcomb Ash to see Angel's parents at Beaminster. She stops to breakfast here. 'Not at the Sow-and-Acorn, for she avoids inns, but at a cottage by the church'. You come to the inn, the church and the cottage to which Hardy refers, to the right of the road. The church is interesting and we discovered that the poet, George Crabbe, was rector from 1783–87. Hardy records his admiration for a writer who, like himself, was not afraid of realism. Crabbe was ahead of his time in that he refused to adopt the fashionable pretence that the villager's life was one of healthy labour and good, if plain, fare. He writes in *The Village*:

> 'Go then, and see them rising with the sun,
> Through a long course of daily toil to run,
> Like him to make the plenteous harvest grow,
> And yet not share the plenty they bestow...'

Hardy also admired Crabbe's technique, what he called his 'novel, good microscopic touch. He gives surface without outline, describing his church by telling *the colour of the lichens*'.

Turn right down Back Lane which runs between the church and Tess Cottage. About a hundred yards down the lane, behind the church is St John's Well, thought to be the source of the river Frome. Close by is the barn where Tess heard the converted Alec d'Urberville preach. Follow the lane round the back of the village to meet the minor road again in front of 'The Common'. Turn left and retrace your steps towards the park gates. Before you come to the gates, the road forks. Now follow the right-hand lane up the hill into the woods. At the top of the hill you walk through a glade of old oaks to see the valley open before you. Across the meadows, copses and thick stands of chestnut trees, you can see the steep slopes of Bubb Down. Follow the path into the valley. At the T-junction turn right, over a stream, then follow the path as it bears left through a gate with a wood on your right. When the wood ceases, the path swings right, then left to meet the main road, the A37, over the meadow ahead. (Ignore the track on the left). Our right of way leads up the meadow from the point where the lane turns right to meet the A37. However, at the time of writing no path is visible. By permission of the landowner, the public are allowed to follow the lane, and you may prefer to do so. You come to the main road through a gate, close to a milestone at the foot of Bubb Down.

Turn left and walk along the wide grass verge beside the road for about a quarter of a mile. Just past a lay-by on the left, you will see a gate on the right opening onto a track. Go right, through the gate and follow the track uphill with a wood on your left. Through the next gate the path divides. Bear left here (this is important!) and walk through the wood and uphill to a gate which leads you into a field high up on the slopes of Bubb Down.

This was a favourite walk of Hardy's. One September evening in 1888 he wrote: 'In the afternoon by train to Eveshot. Walked to Woolcombe, a property once owned by a branch of the Hardy's ... on by the lane and path to Bubb Down'. Woolcombe Farm lies in the valley to the left. You leave the wood to find yourself standing on the open hillside with a magnificent view of the Blackmore Vale spread at your feet. Hardy's note continues, 'Looking east you see High Stoy and the escarpment below it. The Vale of Blackmore is almost entirely green, every hedge being studded with trees. On the left you can see to an immense distance, including Shaftesbury'. In *The Woodlanders* Melbury brings Grace here, to 'Rubdon Hill' as Hardy calls the hillside. He points out to her Dungeon Hill which rises 'out of the level like a great whale'.

An avenue of fine beech trees runs like a mane down the crest of the escarpment on your right. Walk downhill beside them to a gate on the right, then through the gate to continue down the field to Melbury Bubb. The tiny church is one of Dorset's treasures. Still lit by shiny brass oil lamps, it has a beaker-shaped Saxon font with upside down carvings of a dragon and hounds chasing deer and some beautiful fifteenth-century stained glass. The figures are drawn with the grace and delicacy of an illuminated manuscript and they still glow with colour.

Retrace your steps back over Bubb Down to the A37. Turn right and walk along the road for about quarter of a mile until you come to a lane on your left signed for Melbury House, a right of way into Melbury Park. Follow the lane, past the lodge, over the cattle grid until you meet the original path we followed through the park at the beginning of the walk. Turn right to walk back to Melbury Osmond. As I came up the village street I met a retired farmer with his dog. He walked firmly, missing no detail of the autumn countryside. 'I's born in Darset – reckon I's'll die in Darset', he remarked. You could just hear Hardy's woodlander, old Timothy Tangs, commenting on Grace's expensive education, 'When you've got a maid of yer own, John Upjohn, that costs 'ee what she costs him, that will take the squeak out of your Sunday shoes, John!' The accents were the same.

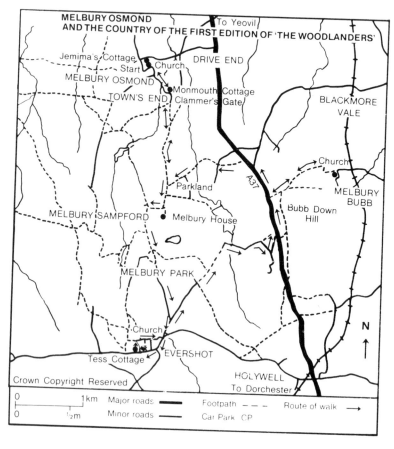

THE WALK IN BRIEF
Distance: about eight miles.

From Dorchester take the A37 road towards Yeovil. Take the left turn for Melbury Osmond and park on the south side of the church. Walk round the tower to see Hardy's mother's home. Then from church walk down the village to Town's End, then right through Clammer's gate into Melbury Osmond Park. In front of house turn right, through park and park gates and down lane to turn right in front of 'The Common' to visit Evershot. Turn right past the church and round village to minor road again. Retrace steps towards the park gates. Before you come to the gates turn right at fork, uphill, then down the valley to main road, A37. Turn left along main road until you come to a lay-by on the left. Opposite is a footpath running right, uphill beside a wood. Path divides, take left path. Follow this to top of Bubb Down. Follow line of beech trees down to gate on right then through gate and down field to Melbury Bubb. Retrace route back to A37. Turn right along road to turning on left, right of way past lodge into Melbury Park. Follow road until it meets original path through the Park. Turn right to walk back to Melbury Osmond.

13

Cerne Abbas and 'The Woodlanders'

Walk distance: about 7 miles

Hardy frequently revised his novels for later editions. In the case of *The Woodlanders* for reasons which he never disclosed, he changed certain topographical details so that the villages of 'Great' and 'Little Hintock' now lay some four or five miles east of the Melburys where the southern fringe of the Blackmore Vale is bordered by High Stoy. Few changes were necessary and the atmosphere of the story is scarcely affected as these communities share common characteristics: their seclusion, their woodlands and the shelter of the chalk hills. Perhaps it was because of this that Hardy never troubled to be very precise about the exact location of Little Hintock.

High Stoy was one of Hardy's favourite view points. He enjoyed cycling and he must have come this way many times. He would follow the valley of the Cerne north from Dorchester through Cerne Abbas and Minterne Magna, then up the incline beyond to where the road takes a lower course between High Stoy and Dogbury Hill before descending into the Blackmore Vale and continuing to Sherborne.

When he could no longer cycle so far, Hardy found other means to reach this favoured spot. In August, 1922, he writes, 'Motored to Sturminster Newton and back by Dogbury Gate. Walked to the top of High Stoy ... thence back home.' He once remarked that *The Woodlanders* was his favourite story adding, 'Perhaps that is owing to the locality and scenery of the action, a part I am very fond of'. Below the chalk hills the vale still lies beneath what Hardy called its 'languorous blue mist'. It is still a country of woods, scattered apple orchards and snug homesteads.

We begin and end our walk in Cerne Abbas – Hardy's 'Abbot's Cernel' – surely one of the most beautiful Dorset villages. We walk along the hillside above the Cerne to High Stoy with marvellous views of the Blackmore Vale and return down another valley, dominated by a medieval manor.

From Dorchester's Top o' Town roundabout, take the A37 Yeovil road. After about a mile and a half the road forks. Turn right along the A352 to Sherborne. The road runs along the valley of the Cerne. On each side the smoothness of the hills is broken by ridges and embankments to show remains of 2000-year-old villages and field systems. You will see more sites of ancient forts, farms and communities on this walk. As the road leaves Godmanstone, look for the thatched Smith's Arms on the right. This is said to be the smallest public house in England. About two miles further, where the Cerne branches to form two shallow valleys, lies Cerne Abbas, a compact cluster of thatched and slate roofs about the fifteenth-century tower of St Mary's Church. Drive past the first turn on the right to the village and continue for about a quarter of a mile until you see on the right a lane from the village joining our road, with the huge white outlined figure of the famous Cerne Abbas giant carved out of the hill directly on your right. Turn right and park in the lay-by in front of Giant Hill.

Ahead, you now have a wonderful view of the rather threatening figure of the giant, straddling the hillside and brandishing his hundred and twenty foot long club as vigorously today as when our Iron Age ancestors carved his outline out of the turf. This huge figure, over 180 feet high, is still something of a mystery. He is believed to have been carved during the Roman occupation, or even earlier. On Giant Hill behind him is plentiful evidence of Iron Age settlements. Is his eminently virile figure meant as a representation of the Emperor Commodus, who declared himself the reincarnation of Hercules in AD 191? Or was he more native in origin, perhaps a Celtic fertility God? Whatever he was, he exercised a strong hold over the imaginations of the local people. He became a folklore character and until recent years was the centre of mid-summer rites. Hardy tells us that at the time of the expected French invasion of the Wessex coast, it was rumoured that 'Boney' lived on human flesh, and ate 'rashers o' baby' for breakfast, 'for all the world like the Cernel Giant in old ancient times'! Could this be based on a vague folk memory dating back some 2000 years to human sacrifices?

From the lay-by walk down the minor road towards Cerne Abbas. Take the first turn on your left which brings you to a bridge over the Cerne. Before the bridge, turn right to walk along the streamside. Go left over the next bridge, then down Mill Lane to emerge in Abbey Street, with the millpond complete with ducks ahead. Our way is left here, but you may prefer to explore one of the loveliest parts of Cerne Abbas first. If so, turn right along Abbey Street which is charming with its row of black and white cottages over-hanging worn flagstones. Facing them is the church of St Mary. Walk round to the south porch to see the gargoyle with a gaping mouth at the side of it. This allowed the smoke to escape from a small hearth which warmed those attending parish meetings inside. The chancel dates from the thirteenth century and is ornamented with fourteenth century wall paintings.

The Benedictine abbey which gave the village the second half of its name, was established in this quiet valley beside the Cerne in AD 987. It flourished until its dissolution in 1539.

To continue our walk, turn left towards the Abbey ruins. Walk down the narrow lane beside the large house that faces down Abbey Street, to the ruins romantically surrounded by trees and gardens. The most striking remains are the four-teenth-century guesthouse which is roofed, and part of the gatehouse which has a lovely oriel window. In his collection of short stories which Hardy calls *A Group of Noble Dames* he includes the tale of *The First Countess of Wessex*. Betty Dornell meets her secret lover, Stephen Reynard, in the 'ruined chamber' of the gatehouse. A charming legend which Hardy tells in his poem *The Lost Pyx* concerns a monk from the abbey. Late one very wet and stormy night, the monk is

Cerne Abbas – Hardy's 'Abbot's Cernel' – cradled in the Dorset downs, seen from the terraced hillside of Giant Hill.

aroused and asked to take the last sacraments to a dying man in the Blackmore Vale. The monk hurries over the hilly ridge behind the abbey, to discover when he is nearly at his destination that he has dropped the pyx which contained the blessed bread, somewhere on his journey. He looks back and, on top of the hill above Batcombe, he sees a brilliant light. When he arrives at the spot, there is the lost pyx surrounded by a reverent circle of wild animals. He hurries back and is just in time to administer the sacraments to the dying man. In gratitude, the monk had the pillar, which you can still see today, known as 'The Cross in Hand', erected on the spot where he found the pyx. The pillar has quite different connotations in *Tess of the d'Urbervilles*. Alex pursues Tess and makes her put her hand on it and swear she will never tempt him with her beauty again. Alec goes on his way to 'Abbots

Cernel' by a path which is possibly the same as ours, and Tess meets a shepherd. He tells her the pillar was never a cross but 'a thing of ill-omen', marking the place where an evil doer was buried. 'They say he sold his soul to the devil, and that he walks at times'.

From the abbey ruins, return down the lane to Abbey Street. On your left you will see an iron gate into the graveyard. Go through this and follow the path that bears left towards another gate. You pass the steps and some of the shaft of Cerne Abbas' old market cross on your right. Through the second gate, bear right along the foot of Giant Hill. Your way lies straight ahead through a dip in the embankment you will see crossing the track. When you reach the dip and the trees are close on your left look carefully left through the trees and a little uphill for a small wooden stile. Turn left and cross the stile. Now turn immediately right along the good path beside the fence, skirting the hill. Bear right at the fork to a wider, crossing path. Bear left and follow this green way as it climbs uphill at first through trees. It may be muddy and overgrown in places but this is only for a few yards. Soon the path leaves the trees and becomes a beautiful terrace leading you gradually up the side of Giant Hill above Yelcombe Bottom. As we climbed the hill in the late October sunshine we were accompanied all the way by the mellow chimes of St Mary's sixteenth and seventeenth century bells. From the height, as you look back, the village seems very small, cupped within the green swell of the downs. Far away on the horizon you can see the Hardy monument.

When the path levels, keep straight on along the top of the field with a hedge on your left to the next gate. Go through and turn immediately left following the arrow bridleway sign through another gate. Walk across the field ahead. Just before a small wood, turn right following the sign along the crest of the hill. Continue to meet a minor road.

Turn left and walk beside the road for about a quarter of a mile. The road swings closer to the steep valley slopes

The Cerne Abbas giant, straddling the hillside and brandishing his hundred and twenty foot club as vigorously today as when the people of the Iron Age carved his outline out of the turf.

and leads through an oak wood. Our path leads from a small wooden gate, to the left of the road, at the end of the wood. (Another path leads right from the opposite side of the road.) Go through the gate and turn right to walk along the brow of the hillside above the Cerne. The valley is beautiful with its rounded copses and graceful sloping meadows. Hidden among the trees is the village of Minterne Magna, sometimes identified with Great Hintock. But the impressive towers of Minterne House are clearly visible, surrounded by gardens and dense woods. Continue along the edge of the field with a fence on your left. Parts of old forest, massive oaks and beeches, now shade our path – we are approaching the country of *The Woodlanders*.

Another gate leads to a good track running along the crest of Little Minterne Hill. Turn left and walk along one of the most beautiful ways in all Wessex. You walk along a high, narrow ridge dividing sharply contrasting countryside. On the right, from the foot of the hillside spreads the little world of the Blackmore Vale, entirely different from the gentle river valley which dips away from you on your left. The ridge narrows further to give even more extensive views of the vale and the remaining dense woodlands around the villages sheltered by the hills. At the time Hardy set *The Woodlanders* here, the area was much more heavily wooded but enough survive to remind us of the importance of the trees in the story.

The whole society of the woodlanders is linked with trees, as the title of the novel suggests. Melbury is a timber merchant, Giles Winterborne travels with his cider press. Melbury's various aches and pains are caused by working in the woods, Giles looks 'like autumn's very brother'. Like *Far from the Madding Crowd* the story is concerned with the effect on this settled society of newcomers who have no connection with, or sympathy for, the old ways. Felice Charmond, the new lady of the manor, is described by one of the locals as not knowing 'a beech from a woak'. Melbury's daughter, Grace, is educated into an uncomfortable position between both worlds. At heart she remains a simple country girl enjoying the everyday woodland scenes. We can look down at the vale and imagine some of these, like the bark rippers sitting telling old country tales round their fire. Or Giles working among the scattered apple orchards in 'the cider country' where 'the air was blue as sapphire – such a blue as outside that apple region was never seen.'

Darker areas planted with pines remind us of Giles planting trees with Marty South. Her love for him is grounded in this shared natural world. This gives her love a nobility that rises far above Grace's more ordinary feelings. Hardy gives Marty a touch of true greatness as she speaks her elegy by Giles' grave: 'Whenever I plant the young larches I'll think that none can plant as you planted . . . If ever I forget your name let me forget home and heaven! But no, no, my love, I never can forget 'ee; for you was a good man, and did good things.'

Tess walked this way on her journey to Beaminster. Like us she looked down at 'the loamy vale of Blackmoor' where the little fields 'looked from this height like the meshes of a net'. Hardy describes her route: 'Keeping the Vale on her right she steered steadily westward; passing above the Hintocks, crossing at right-angles the high road from Sherton-Abbas to Casterbridge, and skirting Dogbury Hill and High Stoy, with the dell between them called 'The Devil's Kitchen'. We are making for 'The Devil's Kitchen' too. From the ridge, follow the path down to cross the A352 over the dell, beneath Dogbury Gate. Carry straight on along the minor road to Leigh and Yetminster which curves through thick woods round High Stoy. Follow the road past great trees 'with spreading roots whose mossed rinds made them like hands wearing green gloves'. After about half a mile the woods on your left cease and the road turns sharply right. Look for a footpath on your left running uphill along the edge of the trees. This is the way. Follow the path as it climbs through the woods. At the top the trees clear. Pass a stile on your

View of Minterne House in the Cerne Valley from the ridge walk along the top of Little Minterne Hill.

Looking the other way from Minterne Hill over the contrasting Blackmore Vale where the little fields 'looked from this height like the meshes of a net'.

right and keep ahead along a grassy track which brings you to a minor road at the top of High Stoy. Turn right and walk along the minor road for about a third of a mile.

There is a public right-of-way to Up Cerne over the field on our left. It is opposite the point on the right where the hedge ceases and there is a field gate with a small track leading from it. On my last visit I found a clear path from the road to a gap in the wood but the bridleway sign was missing. Turn left over the field as as you enter the wood an excellent path leads you downhill through the trees. (If you wish to see the stone pillar called 'The Cross in Hand' continue along the minor road for a little more than a mile. About a quarter of a mile past the right turn to Hilfield, look for the small stone column on the right hand verge of the road).

You leave the trees to emerge in a remote and peaceful little valley that can have changed little since Hardy's day. Follow the track across the field ahead towards the high raised path you will see on the other side which runs close to the hedge along the side of the fields. Now you have a firm wide way beneath your feet and it is easy to imagine Hardy's characters following folk paths like this, along these beautiful secluded valleys. Above the sweeping curve of the fields rises East Hill, a long ridge of tangled gorse and bracken. As we stopped to enjoy the scenery, three young fallow deer were chasing each other merrily around the field quite close to us.

The path meets a lane and bears a little left to give our first view of Up Cerne Manor, a honey-coloured sixteenth-century house. As the lane brings you close you have a perfect view of its long mullioned and transomed windows and steeply pointed gables. There must once have been a larger village here. You pass a fine, eighteenth-century house to join the minor road that runs through Up Cerne opposite the old manor. Turn right, past the manor. Through the trees on the left you will glimpse the tiny church next to the house. Follow the lane to its junction with the A352, a little north of Cerne Abbas. Walk along the main road for a short distance until you come to the minor road to the village, and your car in the lay-by facing Giant Hill.

Hardy probably used the abbey's wonderful fourteenth-century tithe barn as the model for the great barn in *Far from the Madding Crowd*. To see it, turn right at the end of Abbey Street and walk through the village, past the New Inn. Bear right following the Dorchester road for a few yards along part of this road which is called The Folly. Look down the first turning on the left, over a white gate, to see this magnificent barn. One end of it has been converted into a substantial farmhouse.

The Abbey ruins, Cerne Abbas, are open to visitors. There is a very small entrance fee.

Minterne House gardens, Minterne Magna (rhododendrons and spring-flowering shrubs) are shown from 2 pm–7 pm each Sunday in April, May and June, also Easter Monday and Whit Monday. There is an entrance fee.

THE WALK IN BRIEF
Distance: about seven miles.

Park in the lay-by facing Giant Hill, off A352. Follow minor road to Cerne Abbas. Turn first left, right by bridge, left over next bridge, down Mill Lane to Abbey Street. (Abbey ruins on left). Go through iron gate to left of millpond, over graveyard, bearing left through another gate. Turn right across field, to dip in embankment, left to a stile, then immediately right round base of Giant Hill. Bear left up good path, path levels, keep straight on to a gate. Turn left over field, then right to meet a minor road. Turn left along road for ¹/₄ of a mile. At the end of oakwood on left – opposite track on right – turn left through a gate, then right to cross top of fields, through gate, turn left and walk along the side of Little Minterne Hill, over Dogbury Hill and down to cross over A352 below Dogbury Gate. Follow minor road (signposted for Leigh and Yetminster) round High Stoy for about ¹/₂ mile. When woods on left cease, take footpath left, uphill at edge of woods. Follow lane ahead to minor road, then right for ¹/₃ mile. Hedge ceases, gate with track on right, turn left straight over field towards wood, slightly left to gap in trees to pick up good path downhill through wood. Cross straight over an open area to good path on other side, running beside hedge (hedge on right). Turn left as path meets a lane to Up Cerne. Turn right opposite the man to walk to A352. Bear right along A352 to lay-by in front of Giant Hill.

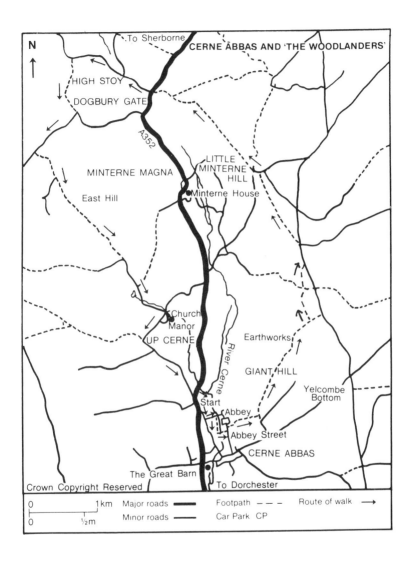

CERNE ABBAS AND 'THE WOODLANDERS'

N

To Sherborne

HIGH STOY

DOGBURY GATE

A352

MINTERNE MAGNA

LITTLE MINTERNE HILL

East Hill

Minterne House

Church

Manor

UP CERNE

River Cerne

Earthworks

GIANT HILL

Yelcombe Bottom

Start

Abbey

Abbey Street

CERNE ABBAS

The Great Barn

To Dorchester

Crown Copyright Reserved

| 0 | 1km | Major roads | ▬▬ | Footpath | – – – | Route of walk | → |
| 0 | ½m | Minor roads | — | Car Park | CP | | |

14

Max Gate
The Frome Valley and
'Tess of the d'Urbervilles'

Walk distance: about 6 miles

As Hardy became more famous, visitors eminent in many fields flocked to Max Gate. But for Hardy, nothing was changed. He continued to find his inspiration in the Dorset people, their folklore, and the quiet countryside he had known all his life. His pleasures remained simple. He records for Christmas 1893, 'Received carol singers as usual on Christmas Eve where, though quite modern, with a harmonium, they made a charming picture with their lanterns under the trees, the rays diminishing away in the winter mist'. Most Sunday afternoons Hardy walked or cycled to see his parents at Bockhampton and after they died he walked over the meadows to visit their graves in Stinsford churchyard. His two sisters and brother Henry moved to live on land which belonged to the family at Talbothays in the Frome valley. Until he was over eighty Hardy cycled the six miles or so down the valley to see them. When he felt he could no longer cycle, he walked. Another favourite walk of Hardy's from Max Gate was down the footpath through the fields opposite his house, perhaps calling to see his friend William Barnes at Came Rectory, or going further, past the church at Winterborne Came to the top of the Downs beyond the Frome valley which look south to the sea. Sometimes Emma would accompany him, but in later years his constant companion was his dog, Wessex.

When Hardy began to make notes for his novel *Tess of the*

d'Urbervilles in the autumn of 1888, he drew for its background on many Wessex scenes. He set some of the most memorable parts of the story close to his home, in the Frome valley. Hardy sometimes calls this valley after the 'Var', the Celtic name for the river, and contrasts the Blackmore Vale where Tess was born – 'The Vale of Little Dairies' – with the Frome Valley where Tess finds her love – 'The Vale of Great Dairies'. After her seduction by Alec, a spurious d'Urberville, Tess wins the love of Angel Clare while she is working as a dairymaid at Talbothays Farm. Hardy imagines the farm a mile or so east of West Stafford. Hardy, of course, knew every detail of this lush, green valley, threaded with streams. As a boy he accompanied his father down to the river and through the meadows past Lewell Mill. Apart from the name, there are other links between the novel and Hardy's own family. Tess's name may have been suggested by that of his cousin, Teresa Hardy who lived at Bockhampton. When the novel was published Teresa said 'the main episodes happened to a relative of theirs'. A strong theme in the novel is the decline of the old Wessex families; among them Hardy included his own.

Our walk takes us in Hardy's steps from Max Gate to Winterborne Came, to the secluded little church where Barnes is buried, across the Frome valley so richly described in *Tess of the d'Urbervilles* and back to Max Gate along his footpath to Stinsford. No area could be richer in Hardy memories.

Max Gate is about a mile south-east of Dorchester beside Alington Avenue which was the main road to Wareham, the A352. Now that the A35 bypasses Dorchester with a slip road to Wareham, there is no need to drive through the town. Approaching from the east or west, follow the bypass signs. Take the turning off the bypass signposted for the A352, Wareham road. This brings you to a roundabout on the A352 which at this point runs almost parallel with Alington Avenue directly opposite Max Gate. Ignore the first left turn to Dorchester and take the next left, a minor road for West Stafford and Crossways. Almost immediately, turn left again past the end of Syward Road and park near the entrance to Max Gate.

Max Gate is a red brick Victorian House. Although it is owned by the National Trust, the house, in accordance with Kate Hardy's wishes, is rented as a private residence. The site is no longer lonely but the house has changed little since a visitor to Max Gate in 1886 wrote: 'From this side the building appears as an unpretending red-brick structure of moderate size, somewhat quaintly built, and standing in a garden which is divided from the upland without by an enclosing wall ... it is evident that from the narrow windows of a turret which rises at the salient angle an extensive view of surrounding country may be obtained'. This visitor found himself greeted by the frenzied barking of Hardy's black setter, Moss. Inside, the house was comfortable and welcoming. The drawing room was to the right of the hall, the dining room to the left.

At first Hardy used the room above the drawing room as his study. Here he wrote *The Woodlanders*. He moved to a room facing west to write *Tess*. Later he wrote much of his poetry in another room looking east over the fields towards Bockhampton where he could see the moon over the pines. Hardy's study has been reconstructed in perfect detail in the Dorset County Museum, Dorchester.

A small wooden door leads from the garden into Syward Road. Hardy had this way made as an escape route when he wished to take his dog, Wessex, for a quiet walk and avoid the crowds who gathered round his front gate. Cross the road to the left of the roundabout with your back to Max Gate. Look directly ahead and you will see a hedge running up the field towards a line of woodland. Walk straight ahead down the embankment following the sign for Winterborne Came to a gate just to the right of the hedge. Go through the gate and follow the path as it runs beside the hedge through the fields. At the foot of a dip, a footpath sign points left to Came Rectory, a pink-washed thatched cottage beside the Wareham Road.

Came Rectory is about half-way between the two villages of Winterborne Came and Whitcombe. It became the house of William Barnes when he left teaching and was appointed rector of both parishes in 1862. When Hardy visited him, in the October following their arrival at Max Gate, Hardy records that they 'talked of old families'. Perhaps Hardy mentioned more of the ideas he was to develop in *Tess*. But the following October Hardy walked this way with sad steps, on his way to attend Barnes' funeral. A touching moment occurred while he was crossing these fields. As Hardy looked across at the cottage – it was evening and the sun was setting – the last rays of sunlight flashed from something being carried out of the porch. The sun had caught the brass fittings on the coffin of his friend being taken to the church. To Hardy this seemed like a special goodbye from his friend. He recalls the incident in his poem *The Last Signal*.

'Thus a farewell to me he signalled on his grave-way,
     As with a wave of his hand.'

If you wish you could make a detour and follow the path to the rectory to see the house more closely. The detour will add about half a mile to the walk.

Our path now leads uphill towards a belt of trees, Came Plantation. After Emma's death in 1912 Hardy mourned her loss in a wealth of poetry, including the specially poignant *The Walk*. In later years Emma had not accompanied him to Came, so why should he feel differently now? Hardy answers the question:

'I walked up there today
Just in the former way;
    Surveyed around
    The familiar ground
    By myself again:
    What difference, then?
Only that underlying sense
Of the look of a room on returning thence'.

But happier days were to follow. In 1914 Hardy married

Florence Dugdale. She records, 'Walked across the field in front of Max Gate towards Came. We both stood on a little flat stone sunk in the path that we call our wishing stone, and I wished'. She recalls another walk when Hardy spent a long time cleaning a tree of a mass of dead weeds that had been thrown into it.

Go through a wooden gate and up a short, steeper climb to the stile just before Came Wood where Hardy often paused to rest. Wessex enjoyed the rest too! Unless the trees are in full leaf you can look back from here and see Max Gate. Cross the stile and walk on through the wood.

As you leave the wood, your path runs down the long, gradual slope ahead. When I first followed this path I walked down an avenue of elms. These succumbed to disease but the hillside has been replanted with beech. From the hill you have a fine view of Came House on the opposite hillside. It is a grey mansion built in 1754 in the Palladian style with a portico and columns by the Damer family. Look to the right of the great house where the line of the woods dips to give a glimpse of downland fields. At the lowest point of the 'V' you will see a small pointed stone arch. This is all that remains of the village of Winterborne Faringdon. The village was destroyed – as an eyesore! – by the Mellors family who at that time owned the manor of Came. Somehow the arch, part of the chancel of the church, survived their efforts. They pulled down a great part of Winterborne Came also but fortunately the church and a handful of cottages were left. The Faringdon ruin forms the background to a scene in *The Trumpet Major* when Anne Garland, certain Bob no longer cares for her, offers her affections to his brother John Loveday.

After the death of his beloved wife Julia, Barnes often walked across the fields to sit in the shade of the ruined chancel.

The track leads down to a minor road that runs through Came Park. Go straight across the road and follow the lane directly ahead. Winterborne Came is completely hidden among its surrounding trees and this secluded valley seemed so lost and remote that I felt we were once again stepping back in time into a changeless world. Follow the track round, past a row of old cottages. We leave the right of way for a short distance here to see Winterborne Came church. (The path is open to public use by kind permission of the land-owner.) Follow the lane ahead for a few yards until you see a sign on the right 'To the church'. Turn right down a narrow path which burrows between thick bushes and the high wall of one of the manor gardens. Keep the wall on your right until the trees and bushes abruptly cease and you emerge to see a tiny stone church surrounded by a miniature graveyard. Close to the tower a Celtic cross marks the grave of William Barnes. This great poet and scholar could not have a quieter or more lovely resting place. His church is dedicated to St Peter. It has preserved its beautiful Jacobean screen with linenfold panelling and an interesting memorial is a marble tablet in memory of a servant, Harriot Voss.

The Frome near Talbothays flowing through the meadows where Tess walked with Angel Clare 'by creeping paths which followed the brinks of trickling tributary brooks . . .'

Retrace your steps from the church back to the minor road running through Came Park. Turn right and walk along the Borne valley, past the lodge at the park gates, to join the main road, A352. Go right along the road for about a quarter of a mile. Now, opposite a lay-by, look for a bridleway sign pointing left to West Stafford. Follow the sign left and walk along the edge of the fields with the hedge close on your left. Go through the gate at the other end of the field and follow the path which now runs along the side of the small Winterborne stream. As we followed the bank in late summer, a narrow stream trickled slowly along the middle of the channel under a blanket of white flowered cress. A fallow deer broke suddenly from the hedge on our right and the sky above the thick copse beyond the stream was black with flapping cawing rooks 'beating off a visiting heron'. Pass some gates on the right and keep straight on to go through a gate opening onto a road. Cross the road to the bridleway sign and follow the track through a gate on the right under a railway bridge and round the old rectory to West Stafford.

The church of St Andrew which you see ahead was probably the scene of Tess's marriage to Angel Clare. The three bells of 'Talbothays parish church' were rung for her wedding. One of the church's three bells is dated 1595 and the other two 1620. Turn left along the minor road in front of the church to a bridge over a branch of the Frome. The rich valley spreading west from here is the scene of Tess's happiest days. Compared with her home in the Blackmore Vale, 'the world was drawn to a larger pattern here . . . the new air was clear, bracing, ethereal. The Froom waters were clear as the pure River of Life shown to the Evangelist, rapid as the shadow of a cloud, with pebbly shallows that prattled to the sky all day long.' Grass grows thick and green; all nature prospers, 'Rays from the sunrise drew forth the buds and stretched them into long stalks, lifted up sap in noiseless streams, opened petals, and sucked out scents in invisible jets and breathings'. Among these scenes of Nature's bounty, Tess falls in love and in true country fashion, she walks with Angel during the golden October afternoons. 'They roved along the meads by creeping paths which followed the brinks of trickling tributary brooks … they were never out of the sound of some purling weir, whose buzz accompanied their own murmurings, whilst the beams of the sun, almost as horizontal as the mead itself, formed a pollen of radiance over the landscape.'

Follow the minor road, past Stafford House, to a T-junction. Our way is right, over the bridge towards Lower Bockhampton. Just after crossing the bridge look right and you will have a fine view of Stafford House, or 'Frome-Everard', as Hardy calls the mansion in his short story *The Waiting Supper*. The woods and weir behind the building are still as Hardy describes them and so is the house itself, 'solidly built of stone in that never-to-be-surpassed style for the English country residence – the mullioned and transomed Elizabethan'.

When you reach the bridge at Lower Bockhampton turn left, before the bridge following the sign for Stinsford and walk along 'the embowered path beside the Frome' that we followed in our first walk. This time, however, we are not going as far as the point where the path curves right for Stinsford church. Just before this turn you come to a bridge over a tributary stream. Turn left immediately before the bridge for St George's road and follow the path, at first a very narrow one, that runs along the bank of the stream. (The stream is on your right.) This was Hardy's way home from Stinsford. Cross the bridge into the meadows by a small brick building. Walk straight on over the watermeadows with a narrow drainage channel on your left. Ahead you will see the viaduct carrying the A35 east of Dorchester. Go over a stile onto a well-defined track. Walk straight on under the viaduct, then turn left over a red brick bridge into a lane.

The lane brings you to St George's road. Turn right towards some old cottages which, before their renovation, could have played their part in the Mixen Lane scenes in *The Mayor of Casterbridge*. Planks for poaching purposes could easily have been laid across the stream behind them to give access to 'the

Moor'. Cross the road and take the first left turn to walk up Eddison Avenue. The avenue turns right, but keep straight on up the footpath ahead between tall hedges. This brings you to a railway bridge with a track running down the far side to a level crossing. This was a favourite spot of Hardy's. Florence records, 'In the afternoon we took one of our usual little walks, around "the triangle" as we call it, that is down the lane by the side of our house, and along the cinder-path beside the railway line. We stood and watched a goods train carrying away huge blocks of Portland Stone as we have done so many times. He never seems tired of watching these stone laden trucks. He said he thought that the shape of Portland would be changed in the course of years by the continual cutting way of its surface'. Six years after *Tess* Hardy wrote his novel *The Well Beloved* set on the Isle of Portland. Look across the field in front and you will see the back of Max Gate, forming the apex of the triangle. Follow the footpath straight ahead which brings you to Alington Avenue. Walk over to the main road and turn left to cross the bridge to return to the roundabout in front of Max Gate. Turn left into Syward Road to return to your car.

Max Gate is open from 2nd April to 27th September on Sunday, Monday and Wednesday from 2 pm – 5 pm. Tel: (01305) 262538

THE WALK IN BRIEF
Distance: about six miles. Easy walking.

Park near the entrance to Max Gate. Return to roundabout on A352, leave roundabout on your right and walk straight ahead down the embankment to gate to right of hedge. Follow the footpath with hedge on your left as it leads you uphill towards Came Wood. Make detour to Came Rectory if wished. Keep straight on, over stile and through Came Plantation down to a minor road through Came Park. Cross road and follow road to church. Retrace route to minor road through park. Turn

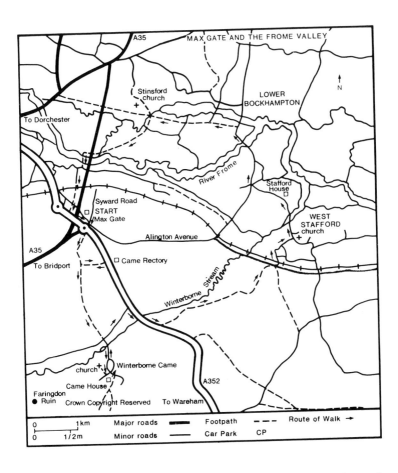

right and walk to A352. Turn right for short distance, look for footpath sign on left to West Stafford. Keep hedge close on left to gate, then along streamside, through gate, over road. Go through gate on right, under railway to West Stafford. In front of church turn left down minor road, past Stafford House, right for Lower Bockhampton. Just before Lower Bockhampton bridge, turn left and walk until just before path bears right for Stinsford church. Turn left before bridge and follow river bank, then across fields, over stile to lane. Follow track under viaduct. Turn left over brick bridge and follow lane ahead to St George's road. Turn right for a few yards, then cross road and take first left up Eddison Avenue. When road turns right keep straight on up footpath, over railway, then straight ahead towards the A352. Turn left then left again in front of Max Gate to your car.

15

Bere Regis
The d'Urberville church
and Greenhill Fair

Walks distances: 5½ miles & 2 miles

Several entries in his notebooks show how concerned Hardy was about the decline in his family's fortunes. Once, he comments, Woolcombe, Froom Quentin, Up-Sydling and Toller Welme were owned by the Hardys. The need to provide for many children sometimes contributed to this decline. He notes there was one partiuclar couple who 'had an enormous lot of children. I remember when young seeing the man – tall and thin – walking beside a horse and common spring trap, and my mother pointing him out to me and saying he represented what was once the leading branch of the family'. So Hardy adds, 'we go down, down, down'. Hardy recalled this remark of his mother's when he made the decline of old families the pivotal theme of *Tess of the d'Urbervilles*. Tess Durbeyfield, apparently the daughter of a poor cottager, is really a descendant of the great d'Urberville family who once owned houses in many parts of Dorset. Her poverty, and the need to provide for six brothers and sisters, triggers a series of misfortunes, beginning with her attempt to 'claim kin' with a spurious member of the d'Urberville family., Alec.

Alec's father is typical of the 'new' aristocracy who, having made their money in trade, bought country estates and with them the influence and social consequence that had formerly belonged to the old families. In Alec's case he had even adopted the name and coat of arms. Often, as was inevitable, these newcomers had no understanding of country ways and folk, or worse, were absentee landlords. This was another of the many contributory factors that were destroying settled country life and its old customs and traditions that Hardy valued. He expresses his thoughts about this changing state of affairs in a great deal of his work but nowhere with greater intensity than in *Tess of the d'Urbervilles*.

The home of Tess's ancestors is Bere Regis. It is easy to rush past its humble thatched cottages without realising that you can still see the remains of its thousand years of history and that close to the main road stands one of the most beautiful churches in England.

Hardy calls Bere Regis 'Kingsbere sub Greenhill'. In the church are the Turberville tombs which he weaves into the story of *Tess*. 'Greenhill' is Woodbury Hill, east of the village. Hardy climbed the hill to make notes for *Far from the Madding Crowd*. The flat plateau on the top was the site of an annual sheep fair and Gabriel Oak brings Bathsheba's and Boldwood's flocks here. South of Bere Regis runs the gently curving and still strangely remote valley of the Puddle river. (West of Puddletown the stream is more often called the Piddle.) The southern slopes of the valley form the edge of another area of heathland which Hardy termed 'East Egdon'. In *The Return of the Native*, Clym and Eustacia make their home here, in a cottage at Alderworth. Today, pine forests have changed the character of their once open heath, dotted only with dwarf oak woods and silver birches and purple with heather in late summer. But, close to Bere Regis, there is an outlying stretch of East Egdon which remains unplanted and exactly as described in the novel. Our walk takes us from Bere Regis, over this lovely heath to Alderworth where the cottage Hardy imagined as Clym and Eustacia's home still remains beneath a knoll crowned with Scots pines. If you wish, you could visit Lawrence of Arabia's cottage at Clouds Hill. T. E. Lawrence often visited Hardy and was one of his most valued friends.

We start from the large car park in Bere Regis. The village now has a by-pass. Follow the directions for the village from the roundabouts on the A35 or A31. Turn left down the minor road signposted Wool and Weymouth. A few yards down this road turn right following the car park sign. You turn right again into the car park.

Before visiting the church, return to the minor road and look straight across the wide expanse of rough grass opposite. You will notice irregular trenches and embankments covering quite a wide area. These are the foundations of a palace built by King John in 1205 and the field is still called 'Court Green'. Across the field the building partly composed of large stones is Court Farm. King John first came here when he landed at Studland having abandoned his idea of invading Normandy. Henry VIII granted the manor of Bere Regis, formerly church lands held by the Abbess of Tarrant, to Robert Turberville and with it the right of burial in part of the church.

Walk up the lane from the road to the south side of the church. Just before you come to the porch are the Turberville tombs with the family vault beneath, and above them a beautiful square-arched Tudor window bearing the Turberville crest, a 'castle argent', and their arms, a 'lion rampant'. Tess tells Alec that her family have a seal and a spoon bearing these insignia. After their eviction following the death of her father, her mother Joan, with Tess and the six younger children, hires a wagon to convey all their possessions – including a large four-poster bed – to hired lodgings in Kingsbere. Unfortunately when they arrive they find the lodgings have been let and they are unable to find anywhere else to stay. It occurs to Joan that their family vault is their own freehold, and they set the bed up beneath the south wall. 'Over the tester of the bedstead was a beautifully traceried window, of many lights, its date being the fifteenth century. It was called the d'Urberville window. . .'.

Inside the south porch two iron hooks, made about 1600, hang either side of the church door. They were used to pull the burning thatch off the roofs of cottages. Fires were frequent occurrences and in 1788 most of Bere Regis, including the vicarage and more than forty houses, was destroyed. The inhabitants joined forces to save the church. You step straight through the door into the Turberville Aisle. Here are the family tombs devoid of their brasses. Hardy describes Tess looking at them: 'Within the window under which the bedstead stood were the tombs of the family, covering in their dates several centuries. They were canopied, altar-shaped, and plain: their carvings being defaced and broken; their brasses torn from the matrices, the rivet-holes remaining like martin-holes in a sand-cliff.' The altar-tomb under the east window is that of Robert Turberville, Lord of the Manor from 1547 to 1559. Perhaps it was on his tomb that Alec lay, pretending to be an effigy so successfully that at first Tess is deceived. This dramatic return of her seducer so saddens Tess that, after he has gone, still threatening he will be her master, she kneels by the large stone slab in the middle of the aisle, the entrance to the vault, and murmurs, 'Why am I the wrong side of this door?'

To leave Tess for a moment, an amusing comment upon some of life's lesser evils is made by the carvings on the pillars along the south aisle. They are ringed by heads; one man clasps his jaw suffering agonies of toothache, while another clutches an obviously aching brow. The carved wood roof of the nave, with its figures of the twelve Apostles dressed as Tudor gentlemen, is the glory of the church: there is no other roof like it in the world. It was a present from Cardinal Morton, who was born in Bere Regis in 1425 and later became lord Chancellor of England, Archbishop of Canterbury and chief adviser to Henry VII. Thomas More, author of *Utopia*, grew up in his household. The date of the colouring of the roof is uncertain, but the churchwardens' book of 1682 records that 'Benjamin was payed five shillings for cleaning and oyling the Apostles'.

From the church return to the minor road and turn right to walk down the road to cross a stream. Beneath are the watercress beds for which Bere Regis is famous. Turn right up Southbrook which leads to Egdon Close. The road bears

The south porch of the church at Bere Regis – Hardy's 'Kingsbere' – leading into the Turberville chapel. In Tess of the d'Urbervilles *it occurs to Tess's mother, Joan, that their family vault is their freehold and as they are homeless she places their bed to the right of the porch beneath 'the d'Urberville window' shown in the photograph.*

left. Ignore a footpath sign and stile on the right. When the road swings right again, carry straight on up the footpath ahead in the direction of Black Hill. The path climbs gently between high hedges which break occasionally to give wide views. Ahead, a little to the right, are the bracken-covered slopes of the out-lying part of East Egdon that remains as Hardy saw it. Just past a joining path on the right, the hedges cease and you come to the bottom of a tree-covered slope, hollowed out in places so that the path is obscured. Do not turn sharp right by the fence, but bear half-right to the highest point between two oak trees. Our path runs just to the right of a small ravine. A blue arrow and some blue and red blazes on the trees roughly indicate our way. Follow the path as it bears a little right to the top. Now you will see

The beautiful 'd'Urberville window' seen from inside the Turberville chapel. Hardy writes 'in the upper part could be discerned heraldic emblems like those of Durbeyfield's old seal and spoon'. These were the Turberville crest, a 'castle argent, and their arms, a 'lion rampant.'

a path leading west through the gorse slightly uphill to the top of Black Hill. Now you are high on the open heath surrounded by magnificent views of wide valleys and distant hills. Over to the left, on a clear day, you can see Corfe Castle in a dip of the skyline guarding the entrance to Purbeck. The wind blows strongly here, scattering changing patterns of light and shade over the gold-brown fern.

Go straight over a crosstrack and soon you come to the top of the hillside overlooking the Puddle stream. Go over another crosstrack and down the hill towards a fascinating wood of old pollarded oaks, their hoary branches twisted into all sorts of grotesque shapes. Through the wood the way becomes a narrow lane, sunk deep beneath the tree roots. The lane bears left, past a farm on the right, to a broad lane at Turners

Puddle. Turn right and walk along the lane through the little hamlet. A bridleway sign 'to Moor Lane' points the way past a lonely church in a terraced graveyard above a branch of the Puddle. Some of the names on the gravestones – Talbut and Chamberlayne – reminded me of the valley's nearness to the Court of King John.

Walk beside the stream until the lane joins the minor road north of Briantspuddle. When you reach the road, turn left and follow it towards the village. You cross the Puddle by a fine stone bridge. Briantspuddle is a charming village of low, heavily-thatched cottages, their thick walls supported by buttresses and painted warm shades of pink and yellow. Follow the road through the village, going straight over the crossroads and up the hill as for Bovington Camp. When you come to a fork, go left for the few yards to another minor road. Cross the road and walk for a short distance down the road ahead, again following the sign for Bovington. On your right is a slight rise covered with tall Scots pines, and in their shade, in a hollow beside the road, are two cottages. This is Alderworth, the home of Clym and Eustacia. Imagine the cottages as they looked in Hardy's time. Clym finds his house 'almost as lonely as that of Eustacia's grandfather, but the fact that it stood near a heath was disguised by a belt of firs which almost enclosed the premises.' Today, the heath is disguised by pine forest, but the firs Hardy mentions – tall pines – still wave proud heads above their modern neighbours. One very hot August afternoon Clym's mother, Mrs Yeobright, walks the six miles from her home at Blooms End to visit her son and his wife. She contemplates the pines' storm-battered shapes, hears the moan of the wind through their branches and understands why 'the place was called the Devil's Bellows'.

Our way back to Bere Regis is by Throop Corner which is mentioned in *The Return of the Native*. But you may like to visit Clouds Hill first. Keep straight on down the road past Alderworth until you meet another minor road. Turn right and walk about a third of a mile to a crossing road. Turn left and continue for a short distance until the road to Bovington joins on the right. A few yards down this road is the cottage at Clouds Hill where, as Lawrence wrote to a friend, he could escape from his life as 'Private Shaw' in the Tank Corps, 'and dream, or write, or read by the fire, or play Beethoven or Mozart'. Hardy records Lawrence's last visit to Max Gate in November 1926 before he went to India. Perhaps Hardy felt it would be the last time he was to see his friend. He went into the little porch and stood at the front door to see the departure of Lawrence on his motor-bicycle. This machine was difficult to start, and, thinking he might have to wait some time Hardy turned into the house to fetch a shawl to wrap around him (Hardy was eighty-six). In the meantime, fearing that Hardy might take a chill, Lawrence started the motor-bicycle and hurried away. Returning a few moments after, Hardy was grieved that he had not seen the actual departure and said that he particularly wished to see Lawrence go.

Retrace the route to Alderworth and walk up to the minor road crossing above the cottages. Now turn right and walk just over half a mile to Throop Clump or Corner. (The first crossroads.) This is where, in *The Return of the Native*, Diggory Venn sees Clym's wife, Eustacia, being escorted home by her former lover, Wildeve. Turn left, downhill, for Throop. A few immaculately kept thatched houses make up this tiny village. Follow the road through the village, and round the corner left for a few yards. Look for a lane, signed for Kite Hill, leading right to a bridge over the Puddle river. Turn right and follow this reed-edged waterside path for about a quarter of a mile to where it joins our original path from Turners Puddle along the valley. Turn right and retrace the route through Turners Puddle, turning left just past the farm to climb the heath and down Black Hill to Bere Regis.

Throughout the Middle Ages and after, Bere Regis was famous for its sheep fairs which were held on the top of nearby Woodbury Hill. In Hardy's time it was still an important market and meeting place, the 'Nijni Novgorod of South

Wessex'. It is a short easy walk to the top of this historic hill. From the top of the minor road where we began our walk (signposted Wool and Weymouth) turn right and walk a short distance along the side of the main road (A35) to the roundabout. Cross straight over towards the hill ahead which is Woodbury Hill. With your back to Bere Regis church tower, look for a yellow waymarked footpath sign indicating a path a few yards to your left. The path leads you straight on to the foot of the hill. Cross a stile and climb the field ahead. More stiles lead you over a track to follow the path as it climbs towards a minor road. A stile leads you to the top of a rather steep bank above the road which looks worse than it really is! The path leads you down gradually. Now look left down the road and you will see a wooden finger post indicating a footpath on the other side. Walk down to the sign (about a hundred yards) which indicates 'Bloxworth' and turn right to follow the path. After a right turn the path climbs quite steeply up the side of Woodbury Hill and leads you to a smooth grassy shelf. Here the sheep were penned for sale. The great ramparts and ditches which you see are the remains of a Roman fortress which once crowned the summit. Follow the path over the shelf, through a dip in the inner ramparts to a wide green where stallholders sold all manner of goods, and where, in *Far from the Madding Crowd*, the tent was erected in which Bathsheba watched Troy enact Dick Turpin's famous ride to York. So moved were two of Bathsheba's workfolk, Jan Coggan and Joseph Poorgrass, by the death of the gallant horse that they rush to join the band of volunteers who carry away Black Bess's body. 'For many a year in Weatherbury, Joseph told, with the air of a man who had had experiences in his time, that he touched with his own hand the hoof of Bess as she lay upon the board upon his shoulder.'

Hardy describes Gabriel Oak bringing his flocks 'through the decayed old town of Kingsbere, and upwards to the plateau . . . climbing the serpentine ways which led to the top' and the noise 'Men were shouting, dogs were barking . . . but the thronging travellers in so long a journey had grown nearly indifferent to such terrors, though they still bleated piteously at the unwontedness of their experiences, a tall shepherd rising here and there in the midst of them, like a gigantic idol amid a crowd of prostrate devotees'.

Retrace your steps down the hill to the minor road again. Our path from the road can be quite difficult to find, so retrace your steps, turning left up the road and look for a wooden stile on the left. Our path is just before the stile leading up the steep bank on your right. A pleasant walk downhill brings you quickly back to the village.

Today, Bere Regis sleeps in its quiet valley. But with Hardy to guide us, we can recapture much of the exciting atmosphere of Bere Regis in earlier days – its great families, its fairs and its markets.

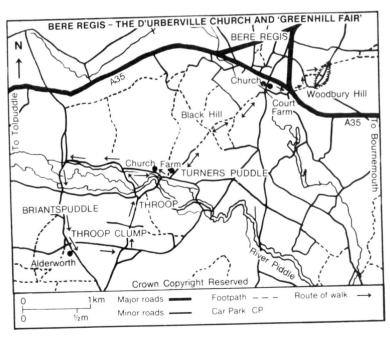

THE WALKS IN BRIEF – *see next page*

THE WALKS IN BRIEF *(see previous page)*
WALK 1. Distance: about five and a half miles. (Extra two miles to visit Clouds Hill.)

Park in car park, Bere Regis. Return to minor road (Wool and Weymouth). Visit the church, then turn right down the minor road to cross a stream. Turn right up Southbrook leading to Egdon Close, then follow footpath straight on when road bends right. When hedges cease at foot of tree-covered slope, bear right for highest point. Then follow good path straight on, over two crosstracks and down hill, bearing left round farm to lane at Turners Puddle. Turn right, past church and follow lane to minor road just north of Briantspuddle. Turn left, walk up through village, over crossroads, left at fork to another minor road. Cross it and keep straight on, following sign to Bovington Camp. Just past this corner is 'Alderworth', beneath pine knoll. (Follow signs to Bovington to visit Clouds Hill.) Return to minor road above Adlerworth. Turn right to Throop Corner, then left down to Throop. Turn left onto minor road for only a few yards then turn right along footpath leading over river to join the original path to Turners Puddle. Return as original route to Bere Regis.

WALK 2. Distance: about two miles. Easy Climb.
To see Woodbury Hill, turn right along A35 from the top of the minor road (Wool and Weymouth). Cross over roundabout and follow footpath straight ahead up the hill. At minor road turn left one hundred yards, then right following sign 'Bloxworth'. Path turns right then leads to the top of the hill. Retrace your steps back to Bere Regis.

16

Wessex Heights – around Melcombe Bingham

Walk distance: about 9 miles

When the village folk in Hardy's stories wished to visit members of their family or friends who lived a distance away or seek work in another area they usually had no option but to walk. Part of a very long journey might perhaps be taken in a carrier's cart like Mrs Dollery's in *The Woodlanders* but for this, of course, they needed money. One of Hardy's most intrepid walkers is Tess, the heroine of *Tess of the d'Urbervilles*.

We have explored some of the countryside Tess knew and contrasted the Blackmore Vale where she was born with the Frome Valley where she fell in love. This walk takes us to the easternmost part of the great chalk upland that divided these areas; to the valleys dominated by the sharp crest of Nettlecombe Tout and up the southern slopes of Bulbarrow Hill whose lonely summit is ringed by Rawlsbury Hill Fort. It was among these bleak hills below Nettlecombe Tout that Tess was compelled to look for work the winter following her desertion by Angel Clare. Hardy suggests the rigour of her life by calling the farm where she works hacking turnips and drawing reeds for thatching, 'Flintcombe Ash'. On his own map he marked a cross in ink about a mile south of Nettlecombe Tout. Hardy's friend, Clive Holland, claimed that the original Flintcombe is Doles Ash Farm, further south. But, like Talbothays, it is better to assume that the place of Tess's sufferings is a creation of Hardy's imagination, built up from numerous separate features of the thin-soiled valleys in this 'irregular chalk table land'.

We begin the walk in the heart of Tess's countryside – from Cross Lanes, just south of Melcombe Bingham. Leave Dorchester in the direction of Bournemouth. Just past Greys Bridge, turn left along the B3143 to Piddletrenthide. Turn right here along the minor road to Cheselbourne (signed 'Ch-b-ne'), then left in the village for Melcombe Bingham. This route shows you the sparse slopes Hardy imagines around Flintcombe Ash. Cross Lanes is about a mile and a half from Cheselbourne, just before you enter Melcombe Bingham.

Park in Melcombe Bingham. Walk back to begin our walk following the lane signposted 'Private Road to Higher Melcombe'. It is, however, a right-of-way and on the corner you will see a bridleway sign 'to the Dorsetshire Gap'. Walk up the lane past a yellow arrow footpath sign on the right, deep into a quiet valley. After about three quarters of a mile, look for a bridleway sign pointing right, before some farm buildings, 'to Melcombe Park'. Turn right as the sign indicates. Our path is directly ahead over Nordon Hill. From the gate, walk up the meadow beside the hedge towards the terraced hillside. At the top of the field go through the gate and follow the good track bearing a little left and cutting deep into the chalk of the hill. As the path leads higher, look south-west over the valleys beneath Nettlecombe Trout, the area of Flintcombe Ash. They are smooth and open with small woods half-hidden in the hollows.

When Tess came to these uplands, the heights, ironically enough, seemed friendly. 'In the middle distance ahead of her she could see the summits of Bulbarrow and Nettlecombe Tout...They had a low and unassuming aspect from this upland, though as approached on the other side from Blackmoor in her childhood they were as lofty bastions against the sky.' Here, at Flintcombe, 'Tess slaved in the morning frosts and in the afternoon rains'. It is from here that she makes her epic walk to Beaminster to see Angel's parents, only to be deterred at the last moment. She leaves Flintcombe again one frosty night in early spring to walk home to Marnhull,

Detail from Hubert Von Herkumer's illustrations from 'Tess of the d'Urbervilles' showing Tess returning from the 'Dance'.

Hardy's 'Marlott'. The route she takes 'ascending and descending till she came to Bulbarrow' must have been very much the way we are following now.

From the top of Nordon Hill a wonderful view of the Blackmore Vale opens at your feet. Nettlecombe Tout frames the vale on your left and on your right rise the more rounded slopes of Bulbarrow Hill, 'well-nigh the highest in South Wessex'. This is exactly where Hardy imagines his traveller to be who has approached the vale from the chalklands. 'Behind him the hills are open, the sun blazes down upon fields so large as to give an unenclosed character to the landscape, the lanes are white, the hedges low and plashed, the atmosphere colourless. Here, in the valley, the world seems to be constructed upon a smaller and more delicate scale; the fields are mere paddocks ... Arable lands are few and limited; with but few exceptions the prospect is a broad rich mass of grass and trees, mantling minor hills and dales within the major. Such is the Vale of Blackmore.' Hardy used this description of the vale twice: the first time in a review of Barnes' poems and then, with little alteration, to describe Tess's home.

Walk straight on over the hill, through the gate and down the field ahead, keeping the hedge on your right. At the foot of the hill you will see a farm gate to your left. Turn left, go through the gate, keep ahead for a few yards then bear right through a farmyard to a lane. Now follow this narrow oak-shaded lane as it leads you into the Vale of Blackmore. The only sounds to reach us here in Tess's 'Vale of Little Diaries' were the lowing of cows and the hum of a tractor. After the wind on the hill, the air felt soft and gentle, hardly moving enough to loosen the last gold leaves from the trees in Melcombe Park beneath the crest of Nettlecombe Tout. But, like Tess, who walked this way in the dark, you do not need sight to know you are in a different world. She 'paced a soil so contrasting with that above it that the difference was perceptible to the tread and to the smell ... the heavy clay land of the Blackmoor Vale'. The difference in atmosphere,

View from Bulbarrow looking over part of the Blackmore Vale towards Nettlecombe Tout and Nordon Hill.

Hardy suggests, may also be due to the whole area being once a great forest still seeming 'to assert something of its old character, the far and near being blended, and every tree and tall hedge making the most of its presence'.

When the lane bends right, keep straight on down the footpath beside Breach Wood. This small hazel coppice fringed with oaks is a survivor from the days when so much of the rural economy depended upon timber. At the end of Breach Wood go through the gate and follow the blue arrow bridleway sign. Continue with the hedge on your left for about a quarter of a mile to a blue arrow pointing right over the field. Turn right and cross the field to a small gate. Go through the gate and ahead of you, a little to the left, you will see a group of farm buildings. We aim to join the lane that runs just to the right of them. The right of way now runs diagonally across two fields towards the farm. Make for the gate you will see half way down the long hedge on the other side of the field. Go through the gate and walk over the next field in the same direction. Before the next hedge, bear right towards the farm and go through the gate to the lane running beside the buildings. This brings you to the minor road leading north to Hazelbury Bryan (Hardy's 'Nuttlebury') and south to Ansty.

Cross the road and follow the bridleway sign to Bulbarrow. Keep to the track as it bears a little left. Pass a track on the left. At this point the track may be flooded in wet weather but there is a raised path to follow beside it. The track leads up to a meadow. Keep straight on and go through the gate at the top. We are aiming for the highest point of Bulbarrow – the green slopes just to the right of the beech woods you will see ahead, a little to your left. So walk up the field bearing slightly left towards a gap in the hedge. Go through the gate and follow the path ahead as it climbs steeply to the summit, crossing the earth ramparts of Rawlsbury Hill Fort. As I climbed over the lower embankment a large green wood-pecker came swiftly past me with his distinctive looping flight. I wondered what could have tempted this woodland bird to this treeless spot. A little further on I found the answer. A wooden cross has been erected high on the fort. Part of it is decaying, and provides the woodpecker with wood-boring insects. To the right of the cross the smooth hillsides fall to the thickly wooded combe where he probably lives.

From the summit, you look down from 900 feet over the vale of Blackmore. When Tess stood here, on her way home, it was round about midnight and she 'looked from that height into the abyss of chaotic shade which was all that revealed itself of the vale on whose further side she was born'. But as I stood on the summit every detail of the magnificent view was etched with clear sunlight. As I looked down on this compact, still green world, with its tree-shaded villages and farms and distant hills, I could readily understand why Hardy loved the Vale so much and included this spectacle among his favourite views. Perhaps it is up here that we feel most sympathy with our great novelist and poet who wrote:

'There are some heights in Wessex, shaped as if by a kindly hand
For thinking, dreaming, dying on . . .'

And concluded:

'So I am found on Ingpen Beacon, or on Wylls-Neck to the west,
Or else on homely Bulbarrow, or little Pilsden Crest,
Where men have never cared to haunt, nor women have walked with me,
And ghosts then keep their distance; and I know some liberty.'

Follow the path along the lower ramparts of the fort to the minor road that runs along the crest of Bulbarrow. Turn right and walk along the road for a short distance. When a road joins from the left, keep straight on as for Dorchester. Soon you come to a Y-junction. Bear right here. The road runs downhill to a T-junction. Turn left and walk uphill for a few yards. Look for a bridleway sign on the right 'to Hilton and Milton Abbey'. (If the sign is missing, it is the track leading through the first gate on your right.)

Leave the road and follow the sign through a gate. The path soon becomes a wide way along the top of a bracken covered hillside. Far below in the valley you will glimpse the small tower of Hilton church. Follow this lovely ridge walk for more than a mile, past a footpath on the right, until you come to a gate in front of a ruined farmhouse. (On my last visit only a very small part of the ruin remained.) Go through the gate to meet a wide crossing track. Turn right past the ruin on your left and take the steep track downhill towards Hilton. The path becomes a lane bordered with tangled spray of bramble and hawthorn which quickly brings you into Hilton, opposite the church.

Hilton is a tiny hamlet of grey flint and white-washed cottages with deep thatched roofs of a warm shade of golden brown, tucked so snugly within its quiet valley that its atmosphere of calm serenity seems scarcely affected by the twentieth century. Hardy's characters would be quite at home here. Its name is derived from the Saxon word 'hel' meaning 'hidden', and so it is. And from here, deep in the countryside Hardy loved, comes a modern instance of that feeling for ancient tradition that he said was so characteristic of these villages. When the folk of Hilton, Ansty, Melcombe Bingham and Cheselbourne were asked by their vicar how they would like to celebrate the 900th anniversary of Salisbury Cathedral they all agreed on their answer: 'Give us back our Randy Day!' they cried. 'Things have never been the same since,' commented one local septuagenarian, Decimus Pitman, who, with his cider-drinking companion, former gamekeeper and cheesemixer, Tom House, could recall the fun and games they had enjoyed on that day as boys. So on 10 July the old custom is revived: the men cut 'randy poles' from the hedgerows and chase the women of their choice. Touch the woman with the wooden 'randy pole' and the man can claim his reward, a kiss. According to the veterans, Randy Day used to include a sumptuous picnic under the chestnut trees. It was said that with the Ansty brewery just up the road, not a person was left sober at the end of the day. How the Puddletown locals in Warrens Malthouse would have envied them!

Have a look inside the church of All Saints. Beneath the tower hang some fifteenth-century wooden panels depicting various saints and said to have been brought from Milton Abbey at the dissolution. There is also an exquisitely carved Jacobean pulpit.

From the porch turn right past the tower and follow a path of single paving stones bearing left away from the church beside a row of beeches. This brings you to a lane running behind the church. Cross the lane and go over the field ahead in the direction indicated by a bridleway sign 'to Aller'. The path leads you to the foot of a wooded hillside. The path to Aller goes right here, but our way is straight on, up the hill. Go over a stile at the top, across the field and over another stile to a minor road. Turn right and walk along the road for a few yards. Take the first track on the left which leads downhill in the direction of Bingham's Melcombe. Follow this deep, sunken lane through the woods into the valley. When the track meets a little road on the right, turn right and follow it for about thirty yards.

The road bears right, but go left through a gate before the curve. You will see the path leading left across the meadow to a footbridge over a stream – the Devil's Water. Cross the bridge, and you are in Bingham's Melcombe. This hidden Dorset gem is a delight: just a tiny church and rectory, a sixteenth-century manor house and a scattering of cottages. Beyond the bridge you pass a small stone building which was once, perhaps, a school. 'Feed my lambs' is written over the porch. The rectory stands to the right of the path and is now a dower house owned by the present holder of the manor, Lady Southborough. Facing it is the church. When I went in the flowers were being arranged for Sunday but time was found to show me a beautifully restored seventeenth-century screen and some fine modern carving on a reredos in the Melcombe Horsey chapel, by a local firm in Dewlish. The Bingham chapel tells the history of the family in monuments and it is interesting to find the arms of the Turberville family featured on the hatchments.

From the church follow the lane left, past the manor. The house is partly concealed behind its flanking walls but you have a splendid view of its thirteenth-century gatehouse. The house was built by the Bingham family and they held the manor until 1895. In a speech that Hardy delivered for the Society of Dorset Men in London he referred to a certain Sir Richard Bingham, of Bingham's Melcombe, 'whom Strype calls a brave soldier . . . he fought in the battles of Candia and Lepanto, and was engaged in all sorts of adventures by land and sea'.

In front of the manor the road turns left to lead through the manor gates to a minor road. Turn right and follow the road which brings you quickly back to where you began, at Cross Lanes.

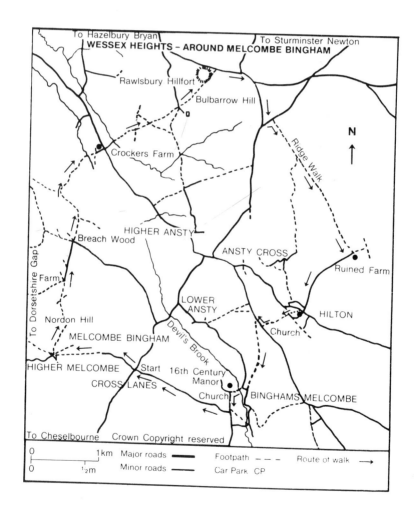

THE WALK IN BRIEF
Distance: about nine miles. This walk includes three fairly steep climbs. Allow a full day.

Start from Cross Lanes. Take road to Higher Melcombe, following bridleway sign to Dorsetshire Gap. Turn right through gate at next bridleway sign but do not follow route to Gap, bear right signed 'Melcombe Park' and follow the hedge straight towards Nordon Hill. Go through gate at top of field and follow path over Nordon Hill, then down the fields the other side past farm on the left to lane into Blackmore Vale. When lane turns right, keep straight on along footpath beside Breach Wood. Go through gate at end of wood, continue for about a quarter of a mile then right over field to gate. Go through gate, then diagonally left down next two fields so that the farm is directly ahead. Leave the farm on the left to join minor road. Cross road and follow bridleway sign to Bulbarrow. Follow track (possibly on raised path beside flooding) to meadow. Keep straight on to go through gate at the top. Walk up field ahead bearing slightly left to gap in hedge. Go through gate. Then follow path to climb the lower ramparts of Rawlsbury Hill Fort. Walk on to minor road across Bulbarrow summit. Turn right, keep straight on at junction, then bear right at Y-junction. At T-junction turn left for a few yards. Follow bridleway sign on right to Hilton and Milton Abbey. Walk along the ridge for over a mile to gate in front of ruined farm. Turn right down lane to Hilton. Cross to church, then from north porch follow path (church on left) to lane behind church. Cross lane and follow bridleway sign to Aller. At wood, carry straight on over hill and down field ahead to minor road. Turn right for about thirty yards and take first lane on the left to Bingham's Melcombe. At road walk a few yards right, then at beginning of right curve, go left through gate into meadow. Path leads left down to a footbridge. Over bridge, past church and manor. By manor turn left and through gates. At road turn right to walk back to Cross Lanes.

17

Portland and 'The Well-Beloved'

Walk distance: about 4½ miles

After the bitter attacks of his critics on *Tess* Hardy offered his editor, Tillotson, a new story which he described as 'something light' to be serialised in the *Illustrated London News* at the close of 1892. This was *The Well-Beloved* which Hardy rewrote for publication in novel form in 1897. But although the theme of *The Well-Beloved* could never provoke the kind of controversy that raged around *Tess* it is far from being 'light' in a trivial sense. The story may seem too unlikely to be taken seriously, but Hardy is in sombre mood as he underlines its message: the power of time to destroy man, his hopes and his ambitions.

In all his novels and many of his poems, Hardy is haunted by a strong sense of time constantly slipping away and the effect of age on himself and others. He sees the power of time's destructive force over man as swift and devastating and he highlights man's position by placing him against a background that, by comparison, appears little affected by time's passing. In *The Return of the Native* Egdon Heath assumes a grim character all its own which dominates all who come within its boundaries. But the strangest of all Hardy's settings is the Isle of Portland, whose brooding, almost sinister presence he suggests with a wealth of animal imagery in *The Well-Beloved*. The sea and wind may buffet this 'Gibraltar of Wessex' as its dark shape stretches 'like the head of a bird' into the Channel; man may even chip away at its bedrock, but Portland remains, connected to the mainland by only a narrow strip of pebbles, apparently unchanged by the passing of time. By contrast, the island's inhabitants are, like all men, intensely vulnerable to time's ravages. In *The Well-Beloved* Hardy reveals the tragic situation that may arise when time has aged a man physically while his emotions and abilities remain youthful. So the main character in the story, Jocelyn Pierston, pursues his ideal of womanhood – his 'well beloved' – through three generations of Island women, the three Avices, to be defeated finally by time. But his story is not entirely tragic. As a successful sculptor, he captures his vision in stone. His quest brings him triumph as an artist: failure as a man.

Time works against Jocelyn in a more obvious fashion also. He is a victim of the conflict between the old ways followed by his Island ancestors and new ideas being spread ever more rapidly by more widespread education and travel. Jocelyn might have succeeded in his quest if Avice Caro had met him as she had promised for an evening walk after their engagement. She fears he might insist on the ancient Island custom of trial marriage. As an islander, she is self-conscious about the old ways and wishes to appear modern. In this respect she is in the same position as Grace Melbury, but as a descendant of an island people which claimed no affinity with the 'kimberlins' on the mainland, Avice is perhaps even more vulnerable. As Hardy says in his Preface to the novel, Portland tends to breed a strange, visionary race all its own.

To walk in Portland today in the steps of Jocelyn and his three Avices is still to enter a different world, quite unlike any other part of Hardy's Wessex. From Dorchester, follow the A354 due south through Weymouth, following the signs for Portland. Pass the Ferry Inn and cross the narrow strip of water called Small Mouth. Now the road runs along Chesil Bank with the dark mass of Portland rising directly ahead. At the roundabout bear right for Chiswell, then right again following the sign 'Chiswell only'. Just before a notice indicating a No Entry 60 yards ahead you will see a chapel on the left and a small parking area on the right close to a row of old cottages evocatively named 'Brandy Row'. We start and finish our walk here. As you leave your car you will hear the sound that is Portland's signature tune, the pounding of the sea against Chesil Beach. Bear right and climb to the top of the pebble bank through the ruins of an earlier Chiswell wrecked in the great gale of 1824. Even on a quiet day the waves break against the beach scooping up the pebbles and throwing them back with a distinctive sucking and roaring noise. In storms the experience of walking along the bank, even on the sheltered side, can be terrifying as Jocelyn and his new love, Marcia Bencomb, find: 'Nothing but the frail bank of pebbles divided them from the raging gulf without, and at every bang of the tide against it the ground shook, the shingle clashed, the spray rose vertically and was blown over their heads'. They shelter beneath a lerret, one of the local fishing boats, and you will see plenty of these dotted about Brandy Row.

Return to the parking area and walk straight on towards the 'No Entry' sign. Look for some steps on the left and climb these to the foot of a road called Mallams. It is another steep climb up Mallams but the road is lined with typical Portland stone cottages so fascinating that you will need to pause frequently to appreciate them properly. Many are still as Hardy describes them, 'all of stone, not only in walls but in window frames, roof, chimneys, fence, stile. . .'. A distinctive feature is the tiny slab-roofed porch that shades each front door. The minute gardens are crammed with flowers that love the warmth of the sun on stone and everywhere there are reminders of the sea – ships in bottles on windowsills, old ship's figure-heads and steering wheels ornamenting tool-sheds.

At the top of Mallams turn right along the main street running through Fortuneswell, Hardy's 'Street of the Wells'. Soon, directly ahead, you will see a very steep green hillside which Hardy described as 'the massive forehead of the Isle'. At the foot the road divides. To the left what Hardy called a 'rigid mathematical road' runs up to the fort encircling the hilltop. We will turn right and take the route trodden most frequently by the people in our story. Follow the road right for only a few yards, then on the left you will see a very steep railed footpath, the route of the old Roman Road across the Island. Climb this to the top of the hill. It is reassuring to recall that Hardy's characters found the climb steep also. After her poetry recital in Fortuneswell, Jocelyn meets Avice and takes her home to 'East Quarriers': 'They climbed homeward slowly by the Old Road, Pierston dragging himself up the steep by the wayside hand-rail and pulling Avice after him upon his arm'. At the top we keep straight on, but if you leave our path and bear right to cross to the War Memorial you will see the wonderful view that they admired. The Dorset coast is spread before you like a map: westward runs the long ridge of the Chesil Bank reaching to Abbotsbury and trapping behind it the quiet waters of the Fleet, and to the east sweeps the gentle curve of Weymouth Bay. Like Avice and Jocelyn you hear the sea pounding against the rocks in Deadman's Bay far below your feet, making its own particular note 'like the single beat of a drum'.

Return to our footpath and keep straight on to meet the main road where you bear a little left for Easton, the village of 'East Quarriers' in our novel. We are now walking over the high part of the Island, the roads bordered with large stones and the surface broken by quarries. Over to the west, surrounded by its cliff-top graveyard, you will see St George's Church, Reforne, its central dome and tower crowned by a cupola silhouetted against the sea. On a later visit to his Island home, Jocelyn looked across at St George's from here and knew instinctively that the burial he was witnessing 'before the seashine' was that of his first Avice.

Follow the path beside the road into Easton. As you come to the Square you pass Stanley House on your left. It is dated 1760 and has a porch decorated with carved pillars. Turn left opposite the clock along Straits road. At the top of the road turn right into Wakeham. This very wide street contains some of the most fascinating houses and gardens on Portland. Cross the bridge over the old railway (rails removed) and walk past the Mermaid Inn where Hardy is remembered chatting to the stone-masons. Now on your left you come to a colour-washed jumble of old cottages. The end cottage, deeply thatched with dripstones arched over its mullioned windows, is the Caro's 'tiny freehold', the home of the Avices in our novel. The cottage was built in 1640 and was occupied until the beginning of this century when it fell into disuse. Now it forms part of the Portland Museum. You enter the Museum through another cottage, 217 Wakeham, which retains its flagged floor, huge crossing beams and open fire-place. Over the small courtyard behind you enter 'Avice Cottage'. Only the shell of Avice's home remains but you can work out the height of the ceiling by the position of an upstairs fireplace and trace the outlines of the interior walls on the flagstones which are worn by countless feet into deep grooves along the central passage. Apart from a good sized living room with a large open fireplace with a bread oven, there was a small front parlour and a back scullery. The windows are set low so that as he walked past Jocelyn had no difficulty in seeing the second Avice working inside. Across the lane, opposite the cottage, is the entrance to Pennsylvania Castle which, under the name of 'Sylvania Castle', Jocelyn rents to be near her. The castle was completed in 1801 to be the home of the Governor of the Island, John Penn, the grandson of the founder of Pennsylvania.

Turn left along the narrow lane leading to Church Ope Cove, in front of 'Avice cottage'. On the right you pass the massive ruined keep of the twelfth century Rufus Castle. Jocelyn often 'paced down the lane to the Red King's castle overhanging the cliff, beside whose age the castle he occupied was but a thing of yesterday'. Within the keep, the third Avice meets her sick lover and they plan their elopement.

The lane plunges steeply down to an open area overlooking the sea. Beneath you are turf-covered slopes littered with rocks and to the right a tiny cove with a pebble beach, dwarfed by the cliffs. Here Avice spread her washing out to dry, weighting it down with the smoothly rounded 'pobbles'. To reach the cove you must follow the little cliff path leading

Avice Cottage 'the Caro's tiny freehold' on Portland, seen through the arch of 'Sylvania' Castle.

down from the open area on the right. We take this path for
about half the distance. When the path turns left, look for a
stone bench on the right. Just past the bench leave the path
and turn right between high hedges to a good path which
takes you past the ruins of St Andrew's church. This was the
parish church of Portland until 1756 and has stood above the
cove – the only natural landing place on the island – for over
eight hundred years. Among the ruins Jocelyn sealed his
engagement to the first Avice with a kiss.

Follow the path past the church and turn right under the
arch of its ruined tower. Our path now climbs through the
trees in the direction of Sylvania Castle, then bears left,
leaving the Castle on the left, to the road. The Castle appears
still as Hardy describes it, 'a dignified manor-house in a nook
by the cliffs, with modern castellations and battlements'. Still,
as in our story, it is shaded by the only dense plantation of
trees on the island and enclosed within a 'girdling wall'.

When you reach the road, turn left and follow it for a short
distance. Just past the Castle and facing the sea, Hardy
imagines Jocelyn's boyhood home, sheltered from 'the whip-
ping salt gales which sped past the walls' by boughs of
euonymus and tamarisk. When the road divides we turn
right along the road for Weston. Pause for a moment on the
corner to look out to sea over the curling white crests of the
infamous Portland Race. Towards these treacherous waters,
the third Avice and her lover drifted in the boat they had
launched so improvidently without oars from Church Ope
Cove.

Follow the Weston road for about two hundred yards until
you see a footpath sign on the right. Turn right along this
path, round the edge of a quarry, to meet a track. Turn left
towards an old windmill you will see ahead. When the path
forks bear right towards a second windmill, then bear right
again to join a road. Turn left and keep straight on down a
footpath beside the track of the old railway (rails removed).
Cross straight over a minor road and follow the footpath
which leads you past a pretty rock garden on the right before

The ruined church in 'Church Ope Cove' with 'Sylvania' Castle on the clifftop behind.

bringing you to another minor road. We are now in Reforne. Cross the road and walk straight on until you meet the main road through the village at a T-junction. Turn left and walk up the street. Soon you will see St George's church at the top. Just before you reach the church you pass the George Inn on your left. This is a Jacobean building such as Hardy mentions in his Preface to the novel, 'built of solid stone ... with mullions, copings and corbels complete'. Formerly it was the home of the Parish Clerk and for many years Portland's own special form of local government, 'The Court Baron and Court of the Manor of Portland', known as 'The Court Leet' held its meetings here.

Cross Weston road to St George's church which, after the demolition of St Andrew's, became the Parish church of Portland. In the cliff-top churchyard 'where the island fathers lay', Jocelyn first sees the second Avice who so much resembles her mother and who becomes another incarnation of his 'well-beloved'. Turn right past the church (the sea on your left) and look for the entrance to a quarry on your left. You will see a footpath sign attached to a lampost indicating the way. Turn left through the entrance, towards the cliffs and shortly the path divides. To the left is the way to the quarry which is private. Our way is to the right. When you reach the cliff top bear right again in the direction of Chiswell. Now we walk along one of the most spectacular cliff paths in Dorset, bordered in places by walls of Portland stone forming miniature canyons. On your left the cliffs fall steeply to narrow strips of pebbles, ceaselessly buffeted by the waves and over the water ahead lies the Dorset coast framed by the soft blue of the Downs. Jocelyn walked these cliffs in his old age with Marcia, when time, though it had robbed him of his vision, had brought him peace.

The cliff path brings you to the corner of the main road. Turn left along the road for a few yards then leave the road following the footpath sign pointing left. The path involves a fairly steep scramble down the cliff until you come to some houses you will see on the right, so if you prefer, you can follow the main road, retrace our earlier route down Fortuneswell main street and turn left down Mallams to Chiswell. The cliff path leads past the houses to bring you to a good metalled path. Continue along this back to the point beside the parking area in Brandy Row where we began our walk.

Avice's cottage

A 'must' for all Hardy enthusiasts. Open Tuesday to Saturday 10–1, 2–5. Entry fee 20p. The Portland Museum is fascinating. The houses and ground were given by Dr Marie Stopes and they were restored and equipped by Public Subscription.

St George's, Reforne

This beautiful Renaissance church was vested in 1971 in the redundant churches fund and is now maintained under the fund by the Friends of St George's Church. It is open daily 2.30–5 from Spring Bank Holiday until the end of September or early October, over Easter and Whitsun weekends. Or you can make special arrangements to visit by contacting the Secretary of the Friends at King Will's Cottage, Wakeham. Phone: Portland 820210.

THE WALK IN BRIEF
Distance: about 4½ miles but hilly. Allow a day.

Park in Chiswell, opposite chapel beside Brandy Row. Walk right to look at Chesil Beach, then return and walk ahead towards 'No Entry' sign. Turn left up steps to Mallams, up Mallams to Fortuneswell main street. Turn right to foot of hill. Turn right for a few yards, then left up footpath with handrail. At the top of the hill continue to road, bear left to Easton. Continue through village to Square, turn left into Straits road at clock, bear right into Wakeham. Left at Avice Cottage down Church Ope lane. Half way down path to beach, when path turns left at bench turn right, past ruins of St Andrew's church, right past tower and up hill past Pennsylvania Castle to road. Turn left, then right for Weston. Two hundred yards take footpath on right, round quarry to meet track. Turn left towards windmill. Path forks, bear right towards second windmill, then right again to join a road. Turn left and keep straight on down footpath beside track of old railway. Cross over minor road, follow footpath over another minor road to a road. Walk on to meet the main street of Reforne at a T-Junction. Turn left up main street. Turn right in front of St George's church for a few yards, then left through quarry entrance (footpath sign now restored) towards cliffs. Bear right at fork, then right again towards Chiswell. When path meets main road, follow road left for a few yards, then take footpath left down cliff, past houses on right, back to Chesil Bank and our parking area. (Or follow main road and retrace route down Fortuneswell main street, left into Mallams, down steps and right to return to our parking area.)

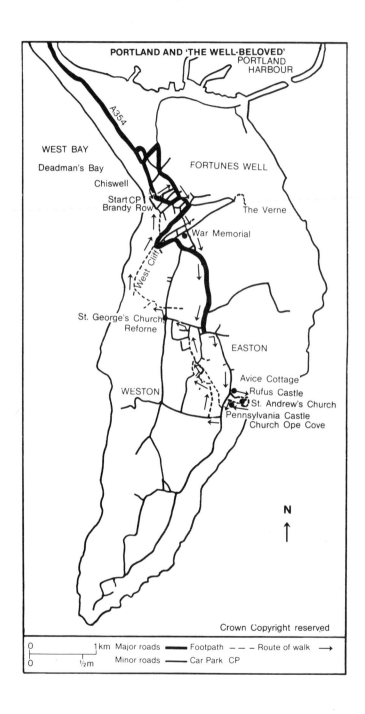

PORTLAND AND 'THE WELL-BELOVED'

PORTLAND HARBOUR

A354

WEST BAY

Deadman's Bay

FORTUNES WELL

Chiswell

Start CP

Brandy Row

The Verne

War Memorial

West Cliff

St. George's Church

Reforne

EASTON

Avice Cottage

Rufus Castle

St. Andrew's Church

WESTON

Pennsylvania Castle

Church Ope Cove

N

| 0 | 1km | Major roads | ▬▬▬ | Footpath | – – – | Route of walk | ⟶ |
| 0 | ½m | Minor roads | ▬▬ | Car Park CP | | | |

18

The North Wessex Downs and 'Jude the Obscure'

Walk distance: 4½ miles

Hardy began what was to be his last great novel, *Jude the Obscure*, in 1892, to be published in novel form in 1895. It is a tragic work; a harsh and uncompromising story written, Hardy said, 'for those into whose souls the iron has entered'. Within this company Hardy would certainly include himself. His father had died earlier in 1892, his relationship with Emma had deteriorated until at times they scarcely spoke to each other, and he was acutely sensitive to the adverse criticism his work received which in his eyes outweighed the praise. As a novelist, Hardy's power to express the conflict inherent in life could only be deepened by these experiences and *Jude* contains some of his finest dramatic writing. Jude himself is the victim of what Hardy calls in his Preface to the novel 'a deadly war waged between flesh and spirit'. He longs to escape from his village background to make a new life in the intellectual atmosphere of Oxford, to free himself from the sexually seductive Arabella who has tricked him into marriage and claim the woman who is his true soul-mate, Sue. He cannot succeed and his struggle brings about his early death. But tragic as the story of Jude undoubtedly is, it is also a tribute to man's greatness. Jude is a hero in the true epic tradition in that he gives his life rather than surrender to fate.

Hardy sets *Jude* brilliantly. With the hand of a master novelist he weaves theme and background together so that each complements and highlights the other. Oxford, Salisbury and Shaftesbury play their part in the novel, but its backbone is the little village of Fawley tucked in the North

Wessex Downs above Wantage. Fawley is the 'Marygreen' of the novel and here Jude experiences 'the chief emotions of his life'. Adopted as a child by his unloving aunt, Drusilla Fawley, Jude quickly learns that God's law of loving-kindness is seldom man's, and that all things give way to expediency. Here he returns at various times in his life when he needs time to recover and think, and when the village claims his Sue, he brings on a last fatal illness in a desperate visit to her.

As we might expect in a novelist so aware of his own roots, many of Hardy's ancestors were buried in the old churchyard in Fawley. His father's mother, the gentle Mary who gives her name to 'Marygreen', spent the first thirteen years of her life as an orphan there. In later years she was Hardy's beloved companion at Bockhampton but, the *Life* tells us, she found the memory of those early years so sad 'that she never cared to return'. Early in 1892 Hardy returned. He walked the paths we shall follow around Fawley and made notes for his novel. As we follow him today, you will see few changes. Fawley is still as Hardy described it, 'old-fashioned as it was small' resting 'in the lap of an undulating upland adjoining the North Wessex Downs'.

Follow the A338 as it climbs over the Downs towards Wantage. Some four miles south of Wantage you will see a sign for Fawley pointing left off the main road. (Drive past the turnings to South Fawley.) The village is about half a mile down the minor road. Drive into the village and keep straight on following the sign 'Bridle Road to Letcombe Bowers' until you come to a green on the left where you can park. Walk along the little track leading left from the road over the green, curving right past a house appropriately named 'Jude Cottage'. This is the site of the village well where we first meet the eleven year old Jude drawing water. The track leads you back to the road again in front of the new church 'of modern Gothic design, unfamiliar to English eyes'. We are following the adult Jude now as, weak and ill, he visited Sue for the last time. Wearing a long greatcoat and wrapped in a blanket he 'crossed the green to the church. ... Here he stood, looking forth at the school.' You will see the school ahead where Sue had returned to Philotson, the husband she detested. Inside the church there was a dramatic scene as Jude appealed to Sue to come back to him. She refused and Jude began his long walk back to Wantage over the down. It is a path he treads many times in the novel and we shall accompany him part of the way.

Turn right past the church and with the green on your right walk down the village to the signpost where a minor road runs right for South Fawley. Turn left here, past some farm buildings and keep straight on along a little lane that leads you towards the down. Hardy imagined Aunt Drusilla's cottage here as the boy Jude was able to run down his aunt's garden, go over the hedge and take this path northward. He

'The pretty new school' at Fawley – Hardy's Marygreen. In the trees sheltering the school are the rooks' nests whose occupants are as noisily present today as they were in Hardy's time!

was employed by Farmer Troutham to scare the rooks off the newly sown fields. Today he would still be needed. Now, as then, the huge beech trees that shelter Fawley are noisy with the cawing of rooks whose black triangular nests are wedged in their upper branches. Just past a barn the lane becomes a green path which leads you through the scene of Jude's labours, 'a wide and lonely depression' in the bare curving downland. It was early in the year and we saw, like Jude, the marks of the plough running up these stark hillsides 'like the channellings in a piece of new corduroy.' No wonder the small Jude feels oppressed by these huge fields which seem to meet the sky all around him. The downs are Jude's inheritance and a prison from which he longs to escape. They are the scene of his suffering also. Feeling sorry for the rooks, whose lives, Jude feels, are as 'puny and sorry' as his own, he allows them to feed, and is caught and thrashed by the farmer for doing so. Far from learning from this experience, Jude remains tender and sympathetic towards those he considers weaker than himself throughout his life, a trait which ennobles his character but, in the circumstances in which he is forced to live, brings about his downfall.

Follow the path as it climbs the down to meet the main road, the A338. Turn left and follow the road towards Wantage, which Hardy calls 'Alfredston' in our novel. (Aptly named after King Alfred, the founder of Wessex, who was born in Wantage.) The boy Jude comes this way for the first time seeking his symbol of a new life, Oxford, or 'Christminster' as Hardy calls the town. In later life, Jude walks this way each week to Alfredston during his apprenticeship as a stonemason. After he marries Arabella, they spend their brief time together in a cottage by this roadside. Continue for about three-quarters of a mile until you are almost at the top of the hill. Before the road bends sharply right, you will see some cottages on the left. Turn left before the cottages along the track that runs beside them. Ahead of you runs one of the oldest roads in Europe, the historic Ridgeway. Hardy writes 'This ancient track ran east and west for many miles, and

The ancient Ridgeway, running just behind the crest of the Down south of Wantage. From the roof of a barn close by Jude glimpses the spires and domes of Oxford – Hardy's Christminster.'

down almost to within living memory had been used for driving flocks and herds to fairs and markets. But it was now neglected and overgrown'. On the corner where you turn along it from the Wantage Road, Hardy places the 'Brown House' (based on the Red Barn which once stood here) from the roof of which young Jude is astonished to see 'the whole northern semicircle between east and west to a distance of forty or fifty miles, spread itself before him' and later, the towers and spires of Oxford in the evening light. From the Ridgeway itself, running as befits a trade route behind the ridge of the Down, we cannot see Jude's view. We follow the Ridgeway for a short distance to Segsbury hill fort to look at it from the ramparts. However, you could make a short detour at this point to see the view if you wish. Do not turn left to follow the Ridgeway, but continue a little further along the Wantage road. If you continue to where a minor road runs left for Letcombe Regis — a distance of about ¼ mile — you are close to the site of the gibbet where, Jude is informed, one of his ancestors was hanged. A little further on you will see a milestone on the right of the road. In the hopeful days of his apprenticeship, Jude carves his initials and 'Thither' on it with a chisel. On his last journey after seeing Sue he spreads his blanket close by and rests. Retrace your steps to the Ridgeway.

Follow the Ridgeway for about half a mile when you will see a lane leading to the earth embankments of Segsbury Hill Fort on your right. Leave the Ridgeway, and turn right along the track which leads you over one of the entrances to the fort, across its flat central area to the northern embankment overlooking the Vale of the White Horse. Now you will see Jude's view. A gentler world of fertile fields, woods and small hills spreads away before you to the horizon. On a clear day you can see Oxford as Jude did. For him, the city shining in the distance was 'the new Jerusalem' offering him boundless opportunities if he could only enter the gates of one of its colleges. One of the obstacles in Jude's way was his weakness for women. From her parents' home in Letcombe Bassett,

Jude walked up to this hill fort with Arabella, before returning to the house with her and allowing her to seduce him.

Apart from his struggles with his own weaknesses, Jude faced external difficulties. The gates of the Oxford Colleges remained firmly closed to Jude the workman, with the dust of his trade on his hands. The world beyond the downs, marking the northernmost limit of Wessex, had no place for him. As you look down from Segsbury, with Alfred's birthplace at your feet, the kingdom of Wessex assumes its special identity and character. Hardy may allow Oxford to stand 'within hail of the Wessex border, and almost with the tip of one small toe within it', but the lush Thames valley and the rich Cotswold hills belong to a different world.

Cross the hill fort back to the Ridgeway and follow it for a little under a quarter of a mile until a track, sheltered by a conspicuous belt of trees, joins it on the left. Turn left and take this lovely ridge path back to Fawley. All around you the hump-backed downs rise and fall, small woods and farmsteads half-hidden in their hollows. Shortly after the track becomes metalled it bears left towards the clump of beeches sheltering Fawley. Walk past the schoolhouse and the church to the green on your right. Opposite the green you will see a gate leading into the old churchyard, which surrounded Fawley church before the new one was built. It has become overgrown but here some of Hardy's ancestors are buried. When I first visited Fawley the churchyard was well cared for and a villager told me that many visitors from overseas came to Fawley old churchyard to see the graves of their ancestors. There were many like Jude who left the harshness of life among these chalk hills to seek new horizons. Hardy would applaud their feeling of kinship.

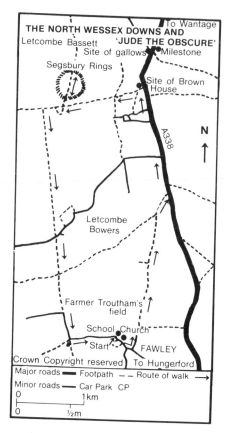

THE WALK IN BRIEF
Distance: 4½ miles.

Park on the green, Fawley village. Follow path left over green, curving right past 'Jude Cottage' back to road. Turn right (church on left) down to signpost, lane on right to South Fawley. Turn left, follow path as it climbs to A338. Turn left along main road for three-quarters of a mile. Turn left before cottages along Ridgeway. (Or continue to top of hill along A338, down to where minor road runs left to Letcombe Basset and little further to see milestone, return to Ridgeway.) Continue along Ridgeway for about half mile. Turn right to walk across Segbsury Hill Fort. Return to Ridgeway and continue. Take next left back to Fawley, following the metalled track left when opposite beech trees shading the village. Pass church and school back to green.

Journey's End

The outspoken views Hardy voiced in *Jude the Obscure*, particularly his insistence that no true marriage could exist if the partners were no longer happy together, led to bitter attacks on the novel. The Bishop of Wakefield announced that he had burnt his copy, an act upon which Hardy commented with dry humour 'probably in his despair at not being able to burn me'. But the attacks, as Hardy wrote in the postscript to *Jude* for the 1912 edition, had the important result of 'completely curing me of further interest in novel writing'. Hardy felt free to turn to the form of writing he really enjoyed, poetry. Outstanding among the wealth of verse he produced over the next thirty years were the poignant love poems he wrote after Emma's death which I have recalled in an earlier chapter.

Hardy continued to write poetry until the November of 1927 when, after being out in a cold wind, he fell ill. On the morning of the 10th January the following year he seemed a little better and asked Florence to read poetry to him. Florence read him Browning's magnificent poem about old age *Rabbi Ben Ezra*. The *Life* tells us that 'she was struck by the look of wistful intentness with which Hardy was listening.' This rally was the prelude to his death, after a heart attack later that day. Hardy's ashes were buried with great pomp in Westminster Abbey but his heart was taken back to the Wessex he had immortalised in his work, and buried in Emma's grave in Stinsford churchyard. Thus the nation paid its tribute to Hardy's greatness as a writer, and the earth of his beloved Wessex claimed what had always been its own.

Book List

Thomas Hardy's Novels and Short Stories:
The new Wessex Edition, Macmillan London Ltd 1974

Thomas Hardy's Poetry:
The Complete Poems of Thomas Hardy. Ed James Gibson. The New
  Wessex Edition, Macmillan London Ltd 1976
A Critical Introduction to the Poems of Thomas Hardy. Trevor Johnson.
  To be published by Macmillan in 1990

Other Prose Works:
Thomas Hardy's Personal Writings. Ed Harold Orel. University of Kansas
  Press, 1966
Macmillan 1967
This is a most interesting collection including *The Dorsetshire Labourer*,
  the Preface to an edition of William Barnes' poetry and all Hardy's
  Prefaces to his own works

Biography:
The Life of Thomas Hardy 1840–1928. Florence Emily Hardy. Macmillan
  1962. St Martin's Press 1962
This was originally published in two volumes: *The Early Life of Thomas
  Hardy* and *The Later Years of Thomas Hardy*. Hardy wrote or super-
  vised the preparation of most of this book himself. It is a valuable and
  indispensable source of information
Thomas Hardy, a Critical Biography. Evelyn Hardy. Russell, 1970
Contains much interesting and original information
Some Recollections. Emma Hardy. Ed Evelyn Hardy and Robert Gittings.
Oxford University Press 1961
Illuminating details of Hardy and Emma in Cornwall
Hardy of Wessex. Carl Weber. Columbia University Press and Routledge
  and Kegan Paul 1965
A most scholarly and readable work
Young Thomas Hardy. Robert Gittings. Heinemann Educational 1975
The Older Hardy. Robert Gittings, Heinemann Educational Books 1978
Both biographies explore with penetrating insight the deeper currents
  running through Hardy's life which had so great an influence on his
  work

Criticism and Topography:
A Hardy Companion. F B Pinion. Macmillan 1974
Just what its name implies. No reader of Hardy should be without this
  book
Thomas Hardy's Wessex. Hermann Lea. Macmillan 1913
Full of fascinating topographical details
Thomas Hardy and Rural England. Merryn Williams. Macmillan 1972
Sets the scene against which Hardy worked; a most interesting book